SUCCESSFUL

Cooking
and Baking

by Ursula Sedgwick
illustrated by Ron Brown
photographs by Philip James

Hamlyn
London . New York . Sydney . Toronto

Useful Facts & Figures

Metric conversion table

All recipes in this book give the ingredients in Imperial units. The table below gives the approximate Metric equivalents (to the nearest 25 grammes).

Solids

Imperial (ounces)	Metric (grammes)
1 oz	25 g
2 oz	50 g
4 oz	100 g
8 oz ($\frac{1}{2}$ lb)	225 g
12 oz	350 g
16 oz (1 lb)	450 g
18 oz	500 g ($\frac{1}{2}$ kilo)

Liquids

Imperial	Metric (decilitres)
$\frac{1}{4}$ pint	$1\frac{1}{2}$ dl
$\frac{1}{2}$ pint	3 dl
$\frac{3}{4}$ pint	4 dl
1 pint	6 dl

Oven temperatures used in this book

The equivalent Celsius temperature used on some electric ovens is given.

Description	Gas No.	Electricity
Very cool	$\frac{1}{2}$–1	250–275°F (130–140°C)
Cool	2	300°F (150°C)
Moderately cool	3	325°F (170°C)
Moderate	4	350°F (180°C)
Moderately hot	5	375°F (190°C)
Fairly hot	6	400°F (200°C)
Hot	7	425°F (220°C)
Very hot	8	450°F (230°C)

Handy weights and measures without scales. *(These are only approximate)*

Liquids

$\frac{1}{2}$ pint (10 fluid ounces) = 1 breakfast cup = 16 tablespoons
$\frac{1}{3}$ pint = 1 teacup
$\frac{1}{4}$ pint (1 gill) = 8 tablespoons
3 large teaspoons = 1 tablespoon

Solids

Cheese (grated)	1 oz	= 4 level tablespoons
Cocoa	1 oz	= 3 level tablespoons
Chocolate powder	1 oz	= 3 level tablespoons
Coconut	1 oz	= 4 level tablespoons
Flour (unsifted)	1 oz	= 3 level tablespoons
Rice	1 oz	= 2 level tablespoons
Sugar (granulated)	1 oz	= 2 level tablespoons
Sugar (castor)	1 oz	= 2 level tablespoons
Sugar (icing)	1 oz	= $2\frac{1}{2}$ level tablespoons
Syrup	1 oz	= 1 level tablespoon

Fats

1 half-pound packet = 8 oz
cut into two for 4 oz pieces
cut into four for 2 oz pieces
cut into eight for 1 oz pieces

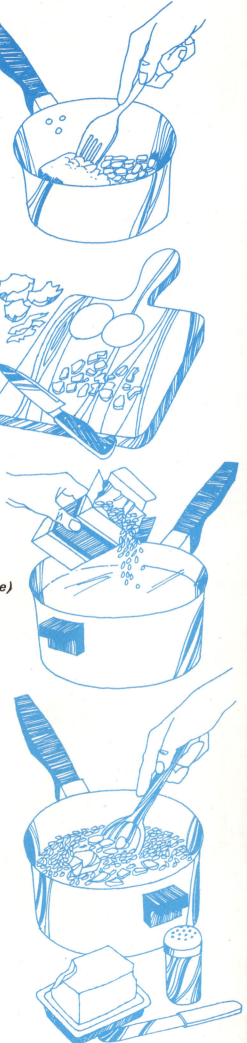

Introduction

SUCCESSFUL COOKING AND BAKING is a book for girls, and boys, who have already learned the basics — how to beat, fold, blend and rub in fat to flour — and who now want to be more adventurous and try cooking interesting and exciting things to eat.

The recipes included come from all round the world and have been chosen because they are fun to make and particularly good to eat, and none of them take long to mix or cook. Small quantities have been given to make some recipes more quickly, and dishes that are for 4—6 people are enough for four hungry people or six small helpings.

To be sure of success, just follow these simple rules:

1. Get all the ingredients out before you start, then nothing will be forgotten. They are listed in the order you will need them.

2. Turn on the oven at the beginning so that you can be sure it will be heated up by the time you want to start baking.

3. Follow the instructions one-by-one in the order given. They are all numbered and difficult steps (with a bold number in colour) are illustrated in detail (in the same colour).

4. Weigh the ingredients accurately, or use the table on page 6 if you do not have any scales.

5. Take a timer with you if you leave the kitchen while a dish is cooking.

6. Wash up as you go along and leave the kitchen tidy.

If you remember these rules when you use this book you can be sure of SUCCESSFUL COOKING AND BAKING.

Acknowledgements

The photographs in this book were taken in the Hamlyn Group Test Kitchen; dishes prepared by Rosemary Wadey; china by courtesy of Stock Designs Ltd.

Published 1975 by
The Hamlyn Publishing Group Limited
London . New York . Sydney . Toronto
Astronaut House, Feltham, Middlesex, England
© Copyright Text Ursula Sedgwick 1975
© Copyright Illustrations The Hamlyn Publishing Group Limited 1975
ISBN 0 600 33103 2
Printed by Tinling (1973) Limited, Prescot, Merseyside

Contents

Cakes

Here are some traditional recipes for cakes that are all made by different methods. Every one will be extremely popular so surprise your friends or family with a tea-time treat.

Try other colours, such as vanilla, chocolate and coffee.

9.

10.

11.

Austrian Marble Cake

You will need:

4 oz butter or margarine
4 oz sugar
2 eggs
2–3 tablespoons milk
6 oz self-raising flour
few drops vanilla essence
few drops cochineal
1 level tablespoon cocoa +
　1 teaspoon water
Mocha Icing (see page 12)

How to make:

1. Turn on oven. Set to Gas No. 5 —Electricity 375°.
2. Grease and flour a 7 inch cake tin.
3. Cream the butter or margarine and sugar.
4. Beat the eggs.
5. Beat the eggs into the butter and sugar mixture.
6. Add the milk and flour alternately to the mixture and beat well.
7. Keep adding the milk, a spoonful at a time, until the mixture reaches a dropping consistency.
8. Divide the mixture into three separate bowls.
9. To one part add a few drops of vanilla and beat in.
10. To the second add a few drops of cochineal. Beat in.
11. Sift the cocoa powder, mix it with a teaspoon of water, add it to the third part, and beat in.
12. Place alternate spoonsful of mixture into the cake tin, arranging the colours so that they overlap and form a pattern.
13. Bake in the centre of a moderately hot oven (Gas No. 5—Electricity 375°) for 40–45 minutes.
14. Turn out and cool on a rack
15. When cool, cover with *Mocha Icing* (see page 12).

12.

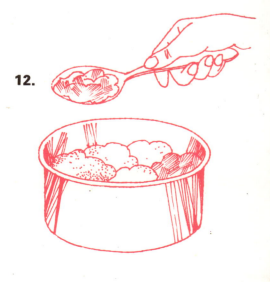

Fruit Buns

You will need:

2 oz self-raising flour
2 oz sugar
pinch of salt
2 oz softened butter or margarine
1 egg
few drops vanilla essence
1 teaspoon water
2 oz sultanas, raisins or mixed fruit

How to make:

1. Turn on oven. Set to Gas No. 5 —Electricity 375°.
2. Grease and flour a tray of 12 bun tins or prepare 12 small paper cases.
3. Put all the ingredients into one bowl and beat together with a wooden spoon.
4. Put one heaped teaspoon of the mixture into each bun tin or paper case.
5. Bake in the top half of a moderately hot oven (Gas No. 5 —Electricity 375°) for 10–15 minutes. *(Makes 12 buns)*

Ginger Buns:

Replace fruit and vanilla with 1 level teaspoon ground ginger +1 oz chopped crystallised ginger.

Old English Gingerbread

You will need:

8 oz plain flour
1 teaspoon ground ginger
good pinch bicarbonate of soda
4 oz soft brown sugar
¼ pint milk
4 oz butter or margarine
2 eggs
8 tablespoons black treacle

6.

How to make:

1. Turn on oven. Set to Gas No. 2 —Electricity 300°.
2. Grease and flour a 7 × 11 inch Swiss Roll tin.
3. Sift together the flour, ginger, bicarbonate of soda, and sugar.
4. Warm the milk and dissolve the butter or margarine in it. *Do not boil.*
5. Beat the eggs.
6. Add the eggs and the treacle to the dry ingredients.
7. Add the milk and butter mixture. Beat well. The mixture should be really runny.
8. Pour into the prepared tin.
9. Bake for 35 minutes in the centre of a cool oven (Gas No. 2—Electricity 300°) then lower the heat to very cool (Gas No. ½–1—Electricity 250°–275°) for a further 25 minutes.
10. Allow to cool in tin before turning out on to a cake rack.

Gingerbread gets even better with keeping!

9

Swiss Roll

You will need:

2 standard eggs
weight of 2 eggs in castor sugar (4 oz)
weight of 1 egg in plain flour (2 oz)
¼ teaspoon baking powder
castor sugar
jam

How to make:

1. Turn on oven. Set to Gas No. 6 —Electricity 400°.
2. Grease a 10 × 7 inch Swiss Roll tin and line it with greaseproof paper. Grease the top of the paper.
3. Stand the jam pot in a pan of water and heat gently.
4. Beat the eggs and sugar over hot water until thick. (This takes at least 10 minutes.)
5. Sift the flour and baking powder and fold into the egg and sugar mixture.
6. Pour into the Swiss Roll tin, spreading it into the corners.
7. Bake in the centre of a fairly hot oven (Gas No. 6— Electricity 400°) for 5–7 minutes.
8. Dredge a damp cloth with castor sugar. Quickly turn out the Swiss Roll on to the sugar.
9. Spread with the softened jam.
10. Roll up carefully while still warm. Leave to cool on rack, with end of roll underneath.
11. Trim the ends before serving.

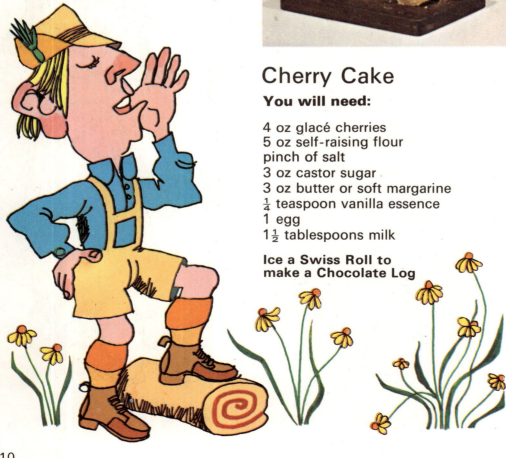

Cherry Cake

You will need:

4 oz glacé cherries
5 oz self-raising flour
pinch of salt
3 oz castor sugar
3 oz butter or soft margarine
¼ teaspoon vanilla essence
1 egg
1½ tablespoons milk

Ice a Swiss Roll to make a Chocolate Log

How to make:

1. Turn on oven. Set to Gas No. 4 —Electricity 350°.
2. Grease and flour a 7 × 4 inch loaf tin (or a 6 inch cake tin).
3. Halve the cherries and toss in 1 tablespoon of the flour.
4. Sift remaining flour, salt and sugar into a bowl.
5. Add the butter or margarine, vanilla essence, egg and milk. Beat well.
6. Fold in the cherries.
7. Pour into the prepared tin.
8. Dredge top with castor sugar.
9. Bake in the centre of a moderate oven (Gas No. 4— Electricity 350°) for 35–40 minutes (or 50–60 minutes in cake tin).
10. Turn out and cool on a rack.

Battenburg Cake

You will need:

4 oz butter or margarine
4 oz sugar
2 eggs
6 oz self-raising flour
pinch of salt
1—2 tablespoons milk
few drops vanilla essence
few drops cochineal
jam
8 oz marzipan

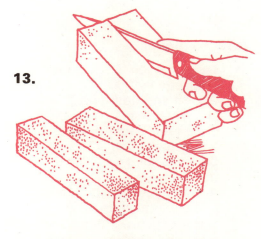

How to make:

1. Turn on oven. Set to Gas No. 5 —Electricity 375°.
2. Grease and flour two 7 × 4 inch small loaf tins.
3. Cream the butter or margarine and sugar.
4. Break in the eggs, one at a time, adding a little of the flour with each. Beat well.
5. Add salt to flour. Sift and fold flour into creamed mixture.
6. Add the milk to bring to a soft dropping consistency.
7. Divide the mixture into two.
8. Add vanilla to one portion; cochineal to the other.
9. Put white half into one loaf tin; pink half into the other.
10. Bake in the centre of a moderately hot oven (Gas No. 5—Electricity 375°) for 25—30 minutes.

11. Turn out and cool on a cake rack.
12. Trim both cakes to the same size, cutting off the outside crusts.
13. Cut each in two lengthways to form four strips (two pink, two white).
14. Warm the jam and use it to 'cement' the pink and white pieces together alternately in two layers.
15. Warm the marzipan and knead it until it is pliable then roll it out thinly into a long strip (7 × 16 inches).
16. Spread the marzipan with warmed jam, place the block of cake (already joined) on it and wrap the marzipan neatly round the cake, leaving both ends exposed.

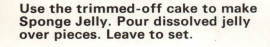

Use the trimmed-off cake to make Sponge Jelly. Pour dissolved jelly over pieces. Leave to set.

American Devil's Food Cake

You will need:

3 oz butter or margarine
6 oz sugar
2 eggs
6 oz plain flour
pinch of salt
2 oz cocoa
2 teaspoons baking powder
¼ pint milk

Mocha Icing

3 oz butter
3 oz icing sugar
1 oz cocoa
1 tablespoon coffee essence
(or 1 teaspoon strong instant
coffee dissolved in 1 tablespoon
warm water)

This cake should be almost black!

5.

7.

9.

How to make:

1. Turn on oven. Set to Gas No. 4
—Electricity 350°.
2. Grease and flour two 7 inch
sandwich tins.
3. Cream the butter or margarine
and sugar together.
4. Separate the egg yolks from
the whites.
5. Add the yolks to the butter
and sugar mixture.
6. Sift together the flour, salt,
cocoa and baking powder.
7. Add this to the mixture
alternately with the milk.
Mix well.
8. Beat the egg whites stiffly.
9. Fold the beaten whites into
the mixture.
10. Turn into the prepared
sandwich tins.
11. Bake in the centre of a
moderate oven (Gas No. 4—
Electricity 350°) for 25–30
minutes.
12. Turn out and cool on a rack.

To make Mocha Icing

13. Beat together butter, icing
sugar, cocoa and coffee
essence.
14. Spread half the icing on one
layer of the cake. Cover it with
the second layer and swirl the
icing roughly over the top.

Coffee Parcel Cake

You will need:

4 oz butter or margarine
4 oz sugar
2 eggs
1 tablespoon coffee essence
4 oz self-raising flour

Coffee Butter Icing

2 oz butter
2 oz icing sugar
1 dessertspoon coffee essence

Coffee Glacé Icing

12 oz icing sugar
3–4 dessertspoons warm water
1 dessertspoon coffee essence

White Glacé Icing

2 oz icing sugar
1 teaspoon warm water

How to make:

1. Turn on oven. Set to Gas No. 5
   —Electricity 375°.
2. Grease and flour a 10 × 7
   inch Swiss Roll tin.
3. Cream the butter or margarine
   with the sugar.
4. Break in the eggs, one at a
   time, adding a little of the flour
   with each. Beat well.
5. Add the coffee essence,
   together with a little more of
   the flour. Beat again.
6. Sift remaining flour and fold in.
7. Pour the mixture into the
   Swiss Roll tin spreading it
   right into the corners.
8. Bake in the top half of a
   moderately hot oven (Gas No.
   5—Electricity 375°) for 15–20
   minutes.
9. Turn out and cool on a rack.
10. When cool, divide into three
    equal portions. Place them on
    top of each other and trim
    them to get a firm upright edge.

To make Coffee Butter Icing

11. Beat together the butter, icing
    sugar and coffee essence.
    Spread between the layers
    of the cake.

10.

To make Coffee Glacé Icing

12. Sift 12 oz icing sugar into a
    saucepan. Add 2 dessert-
    spoons warm water and
    1 dessertspoon coffee essence.
    Dissolve over a low heat,
    stirring with a wooden spoon.
    Do not let icing get too hot.
13. When the icing looks smooth
    and glossy and coats the
    spoon thickly, pour over the
    cake, smoothing it against the
    sides with a wet palette knife.
14. While the icing sets, take a
    plastic bag, and make a small
    hole in one corner (or fold a
    piece of greaseproof paper
    into a *poke bag*).

11.

12.

To make White Glacé Icing

15. Sift the 2 oz icing sugar into
    a saucepan. Add 1 teaspoon
    warm water and dissolve over
    a low heat, stirring as before.
    When the icing coats the
    spoon thickly, pour into the
    bag and use to put 'string'
    around the parcel and to
    write the name and address.

13.

Use this recipe (without the Glacé
Icing) for *Coffee Sponge Sandwich.*
Divide the mixture into two 7 inch
sandwich tins. Bake for 25–30
minutes (Gas No. 5—Electricity
375°). Sandwich together with
Coffee Butter Icing and dust the
top with icing sugar.

Biscuits

Home-made biscuits are absolutely delicious and these four varieties will be very popular at parties. For a special treat, serve Palmiers sandwiched together with whipped cream, and fill brandy snaps too.

The Dutch eat these biscuits on St. Nicholas' Day – December 6.

St. Nicholas' Day Letters

You will need:

8 oz frozen flaky pastry
4 oz marzipan
milk

How to make:

1. Thaw out pastry for one hour.
2. Turn on oven. Set to Gas No. 7 —Electricity 425°.
3. Roll out pastry to $\frac{1}{8}$ inch thickness and cut into strips 4 × 2 inches.
4. Lay a thin strip of marzipan lengthwise on the pastry, leaving both ends free.
5. Roll the pastry round the marzipan enclosing it in a long, narrow roll.
6. Seal edge and ends with milk.
7. Form each pastry roll into a letter. Try I, O, U, J, L, D, C, P, S, Z and V first. Then experiment with different length strips to get X, T, A, H, F, N, M etc. Seal the joins with a little milk.
8. Place carefully on an ungreased baking tray.
9. Brush the tops with milk.
10. Bake in a hot oven (Gas No. 7 —Electricity 425°) for 15–20 minutes.
11. Remove carefully and cool on a cake rack.
    (Makes 16–20 biscuits depending on letters chosen)

5.

7.

8.

In France these biscuits are called 'tuiles' or tiles because they look like bent roof tiles.

Bent Biscuits

You will need:

$\frac{1}{2}$ oz plain flour
2 oz castor sugar
pinch of salt
1 egg white
1 oz melted butter
$\frac{1}{2}$ oz flaked or chopped almonds

How to make:

1. Turn on oven. Set to Gas No. 7 —Electricity 425°.
2. Grease a baking tray with butter.
3. Sift together the flour, sugar and salt.
4. Add melted butter and unbeaten egg white. Beat them all together.
5. Fold in almonds.
6. Put 4 teaspoonsful of the mixture spaced far apart on the baking tray. Spread and flatten slightly with a spoon.
7. Bake at the top of a very hot oven (Gas No. 7 —Electricity 425°) for 3–4 minutes.
8. Allow to cool slightly, then remove carefully with a palette knife and drape over a rolling pin to cool.
9. Remove to a wire tray to allow room for the next 4 biscuits.
   (Makes approximately 20 biscuits)

Palmiers

You will need:

8 oz frozen puff pastry
castor sugar

How to make:

1. Thaw out pastry completely at room temperature.
2. Turn on oven. Set to Gas No. 8 —Electricity 450°.
3. Grease a baking tray with butter.
4. Dredge a pastry board with sugar and roll out the pastry to a 10 × 16 inch oblong.
5. Dredge the pastry with sugar.
6. Fold in half lengthways (giving an oblong about 5 × 16 inches). Sugar again.
7. Fold the ends towards the centre, then fold again. Sugar it at each fold.
8. Fold the two portions together.
9. Holding the pastry firmly, cut with a sharp knife into biscuits (about 10).
10. Sugar them on both sides and lay on the baking tray, leaving plenty of room to spread.
11. Bake in the top half of a very hot oven (Gas No. 7—Electricity 425°) for 12–15 minutes.
12. Cool on a cake rack.
   (Makes 8–10 single biscuits)

7.

9.

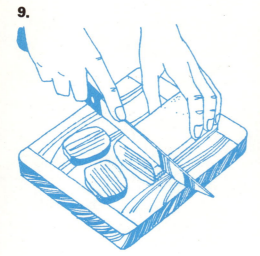

Brandy Snaps

You will need:

2 level tablespoons golden syrup
2 oz butter
2 oz sugar
2 oz plain flour
1 teaspoon ground ginger
$\frac{1}{2}$ teaspoon lemon juice

How to make:

1. Turn on oven. Set to Gas No. 5 —Electricity 375°.
2. Grease a baking tray with butter.
3. Gently heat together the golden syrup, butter and sugar. Remove from heat and allow to cool slightly.
4. Sift the flour and ginger.
5. Add the syrup mixture and the lemon juice and beat.
6. Put two or three teaspoonsful of the mixture on to the baking tray, at least 6 inches apart to allow for spreading. *Do not cook more than 3 at once.*
7. Bake in top half of moderately hot oven (Gas No. 5—Electricity 375°) for 5–6 minutes.
8. Let the Brandy Snaps cool enough to hold their shape. Use a palette knife, to gently lever them off the baking tray.
9. Roll them round a wooden spoon handle. Remove when set.
10. Serve plain or fill with whipped cream for a party.
   (Makes approximately 10 Brandy Snaps)

If the Brandy Snaps harden before removal from the baking tray, put them back into the oven to soften.

These are also known as fairings because, traditionally, they are sold at fairs.

Bread

Not as sweet as cakes but much more filling than biscuits — cut a slice from one of these and eat it when you are feeling really hungry. Wrapped in foil or stored in an air-tight tin, they keep well too.

Cheese Scones

You will need:

4 oz plain flour
$\frac{1}{2}$ teaspoon cream of tartar
$\frac{1}{4}$ teaspoon bicarbonate of soda
pinch of salt, pepper and
    mustard powder
1 oz margarine
2 oz cheese
4–5 tablespoons milk

How to make:

1. Turn on the oven. Set to Gas No. 8—Electricity 450°.
2. Grease a baking sheet.
3. Sift together the flour, cream of tartar, bicarbonate of soda, salt, pepper and mustard powder.
4. Rub in the margarine.
5. Grate the cheese and add to dry ingredients.
6. Add the milk and blend to form a soft dough.
7. Roll out on a floured board into a circle about $\frac{3}{4}$ inch thick.
8. Mark with a knife into 6 or 8 triangular sectors, but do not cut through.
9. Brush the top with milk.
10. Bake on the baking sheet in a very hot oven (Gas No. 8— Electricity 450°) for 7–10 minutes.
11. Serve in triangles, hot or cold, with butter or a savoury spread and salad.
    (Makes 6–8 scones)

To make tiny, bit-size scones, use an egg cup as a cutter.

7.

8.

9.

11.

Bavarian Honey Bread

You will need:

6 oz self-raising flour
½ teaspoon cinnamon
pinch of salt
2 oz sugar
1 tablespoon honey
6 tablespoons milk
1 oz butter

How to make:

1. Turn on the oven. Set to Gas No. 4—Electricity 350°.
2. Grease and flour a 7 × 4 inch loaf tin.
3. Sift together the flour, cinnamon, salt and sugar.
4. *Gently warm* the honey with the milk and butter. *Do not allow to get too hot.*
5. Gradually add the honey and milk to the dry ingredients, stirring all the time.
6. Pour the mixture, which will be quite runny, into the prepared tin and bake in a moderate oven (Gas No. 4—Electricity 350°) for 35—40 minutes.
7. Allow to cool in the tin before turning out on to a cake rack.
8. Serve in slices, plain or buttered.

In Germany we eat this by itself or spread with butter.

Date and Walnut Loaf

You will need:

4 oz self-raising flour
pinch of salt
1 oz castor sugar
3 oz butter or margarine
3 oz chopped dates
1 oz chopped walnuts
5—6 tablespoons milk

How to make:

1. Turn on the oven. Set to Gas No. 4—Electricity 350°.
2. Grease and flour a 7 × 4 inch loaf tin.
3. Sift the flour, salt and sugar into a bowl.
4. Rub in the butter or margarine.
5. Stir in the chopped dates and chopped walnuts.
6. Add the milk a little at a time and stir until the mixture reaches a soft, dropping consistency.
7. Pour into the prepared tin and bake in a moderate oven (Gas No. 4—Electricity 350°) for 35—40 minutes.
8. Allow to cool slightly, then turn out and cool on a rack.
9. To serve, cut into slices or fingers, some plain, some buttered.

Sandwiches

Sandwiches can be eaten on many occasions, for supper or snacks, at parties or picnics. Try some of these exciting fillings for a change. There are some sandwiches that can be served hot too.

4.

Flavoured Butter

Brown Butter: put 2 oz butter or soft margarine in a bowl. Blend in ½ teaspoon yeast extract.
Cheese Butter: Blend in 1½ oz greated Cheddar.
Orange Butter: Blend in 1 dessert-spoon orange juice, grated rind of ½ orange, 1 teaspoon castor sugar.
Tomato Butter: Blend in 1 dessert-spoon tomato ketchup and a pinch of salt.

Continentals —

Each one is a meal in itself

1. Cut French bread diagonally into long boat-shaped pieces.
2. Spread with *Brown Butter.*
3. Arrange a lettuce leaf, a slice of ham and a slice of hard-boiled egg on top.
4. Repeat for the number you want; or vary with *Tomato Butter* with lettuce and a half sardine on top. Try *Orange Butter* with lettuce and sliced chicken or *Cheese Butter* with lettuce and and sliced tomato.

4.

5.

Fried Sandwiches

Use up leftovers

1. Make a sandwich with any filling except lettuce.
2. Melt butter or margarine in the frying pan.
3. Fry the sandwich to a rich golden colour.
4. Serve with a fried egg on top.

Pinwheels —

Perfect for a party

1. Ask for a sandwich loaf of unsliced bread.
2. Cut off the crust from three sides and both ends of the loaf.
3. Spread the top with peanut butter (or any other spread).
4. Turn loaf on its side and cut a long thin slice.
5. Roll up carefully from one end.
6. Wrap tightly in aluminium foil and keep in the refrigerator until wanted.
7. Just before eating, remove from foil, cut crosswise into pinwheels.

2.

Triple-deckers —

All you need for a picnic

1. Spread four slices of bread with butter or soft margarine.
2. On the first put lettuce and grated cheese; on the second put sliced tomato; on the third put scrambled egg. Top with fourth slice, butter side down. For a supper dish—replace the bread with toast.

Open Toasted Sandwiches —

A quick dish for a cold day.

1. Toast bread on one side under the grill and turn over.
2. Cover the *untoasted* side with grated cheese. Put it back under the grill.
3. When the cheese begins to bubble, remove from grill and add chopped tomato.
4. Replace under grill to finish cooking.

3.

3.

Heroes —

For a hungry day

1. Cut a small French loaf horizontally (one for each person).
2. Spread with butter or soft margarine.
3. Fill with lettuce, tomato and cucumber or with *Salad Niçoise* (see page 25).
4. Put together as a sandwich. Eat when *really* hungry.

Other ideas for sandwich fillings:

Mashed banana and cream cheese; bacon and fried egg, coconut and lemon curd; grated chocolate and raisins or sultanas; sardine with tomato sauce; jam or jelly and peanut butter; chopped apple with chopped celery; salad cream with chopped hard-boiled egg.

Soups

Piping hot soup and fresh sandwiches make a quick filling meal. Fill a flask with hot soup on a cold day, for a journey, a fishing trip or a football match. In warmer weather, serve cold soup, well chilled.

A soup from Bonnie Scotland!

Cock-a-Leekie
(for 4–6 people)

You will need:

6 large leeks
1 chicken carcass and any extra chicken bones available
2½ pints chicken stock (made with 3 stock cubes)
salt and pepper for seasoning
4–6 tablespoons long-grain rice

How to make:

1. Trim off the root and green part of the leeks. Wash thoroughly.
2. Cut into slices.
3. Put the leeks with the chicken carcass, and bones if available, into cold water, together with stock cubes and salt and pepper to season.
4. Boil, with the lid on, for 1 hour.
5. Remove from the heat. Skim the top of the soup with a tablespoon. Take out the chicken with a perforated spoon (or pour through a sieve into a second pan).
6. Allow the chicken to cool enough to handle, then take off the remaining chicken meat. Replace the meat in the soup and throw away the bones.
7. Add long-grain rice and boil until this is tender (approximately 15 minutes).
8. Skim fat off before serving. Serve very hot.

5.

6.

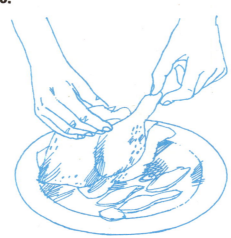

Zuppa Pavese
(for 4 people)

You will need:

1½ pints chicken or beef consommé (canned or made from stock cubes)
4 oz cheese
4 large slices bread
butter or margarine for frying
4 eggs

How to make:

1. Put 4 soup bowls to warm.
2. Heat chicken or beef consommé.
3. Grate the cheese finely.
4. Cut each slice of bread into 4 triangles and fry in butter or margarine.
5. Poach the eggs in the boiling soup, to give them flavour.
6. Place an egg in the middle of each warmed soup bowl.
7. Pour the soup round the egg.
8. Pile the grated cheese on to the triangles of fried bread and place round each egg.
9. Sprinkle extra cheese on top.
10. Serve immediately, very hot.

Vichyssoise

(for 4 people)

You will need:

2 oz butter or margarine
4 large leeks
1 small onion
3 medium sized potatoes
1½ pints chicken stock (or use
   stock cubes)
salt and pepper for seasoning
4 dessertspoons double cream
chives or spring onion tops (if
   available)

How to make:

1. Melt the butter or margarine
   in a saucepan.
2. Discard the roots and green
   parts of the leeks and wash
   well. Peel the onion. Chop
   leeks and onion and fry very
   gently in the pan until soft.
   Do not allow to brown.
   Remove from heat.
3. Peel and slice the potatoes.
   Add to the onion and leeks.
4. Add stock and season well.
5. Simmer for 30–35 minutes
   until the vegetables are cooked.
6. Pass through a sieve (or use
   a liquidiser if you have one).
7. Chill in the refrigerator.
8. Serve very cold. Just before
   serving take a dessertspoon
   of cream for each helping and
   trickle it round the soup.
9. If available, sprinkle chopped
   chives or spring onion tops on
   the surface.

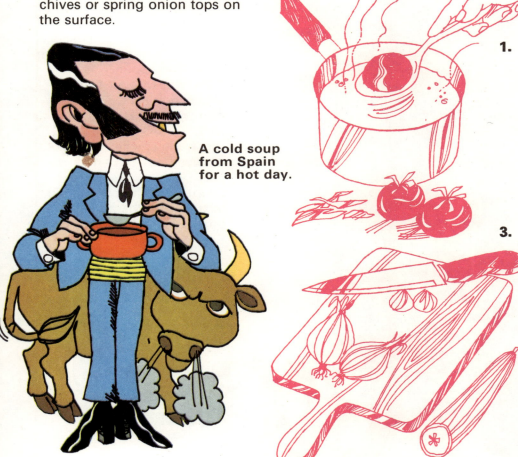

A cold soup from Spain for a hot day.

Gazpacho

(for 4 people)

You will need:

1 lb tomatoes
2 onions
1 small cucumber
garlic (if available)
salt and pepper (ground black
   pepper if possible)

How to make:

1. Remove the skin from the
   tomatoes by dropping each
   tomato into boiling water,
   removing after a few seconds
   and peeling off the skin.
2. Pass the tomatoes through a
   sieve (or use a liquidiser if you
   have one).
3. Chop the onions very small.
4. Peel the cucumber and chop
   very small.
5. Chop the garlic (if available)
   very small.
6. Blend all the ingredients.
   Season with salt and pepper.
7. Chill in the refrigerator and
   serve very cold.

Main Courses

Here are recipes from all around the world giving you a wide choice of main dishes to make for every occasion. Serve them on attractive dishes to make them look extra appetizing. Add a sprig of parsley for a professional touch.

If you have any corn kernels left over, mix with peas and serve as a vegetable.

2.

7.

Chicken Maryland with Corn Fritters
(for 4 people)

You will need:

1 egg
4 joints of chicken
3 heaped tablespoons brown breadcrumbs
oil or lard for frying

Corn Fritters

2 level tablespoons self-raising flour
pinch of salt
pinch of cayenne pepper
½ teaspoon Worcester sauce
1 tablespoon milk
4 heaped tablespoons corn kernels (canned or frozen)

How to make:

1. Break the egg into a cup. Beat with a fork and pour half into a deep plate.
2. Dip the chicken joints into the egg.
3. Coat with the breadcrumbs.
4. Heat the oil or lard (about ½ inch deep) in a large frying pan. When really hot, add the chicken. Turn until brown all over, then reduce the heat and cook, turning as required, for 20 minutes.

To make the Corn Fritters

5. Put flour into a bowl, add the rest of the egg, salt, cayenne pepper and Worcester sauce. Beat to a smooth batter with a wooden spoon.
6. If too stiff to pour add 1 tablespoon milk.
7. Add the corn kernels and mix well.
8. When the chicken is cooked, remove from pan and keep warm.
9. Drop spoonsful of the corn mixture into the fat and fry both sides until golden brown. Serve very hot.

9.

Australian Minced-Beef Sandwich
(for 4–6 people)

You will need:

breadcrumbs made from
  2 slices of bread
$\frac{1}{4}$ pint milk
8 oz minced beef
2 small onions
2 small beetroots (when available)
1 tablespoon capers (if available)
salt and pepper for seasoning
1 teaspoon Worcester sauce
6 large slices bread
lard for frying

How to make:

1. Make fresh breadcrumbs in electric blender or by rubbing through a sieve.
2. Mix breadcrumbs with milk and minced beef.
3. Chop onions and beetroot and add with capers (if used).
4. Mix well and season with salt and pepper. Add Worcester sauce.
5. Fry slices of bread on one side.
6. Spread the mince mixture on the fried side, return slices to the frying pan and fry meat-side-down.
7. Turn and fry the unfried side of the bread.
8. Turn again and serve very hot, meat-side-up.

An upside-down recipe from down-under.

Pissaladière

(for 4 people)

You will need:

1 sandwich loaf
3 large onions
3 large tomatoes
1 can anchovy fillets *or*
   1 small jar anchovy paste
10 black olives (more if you like)
oil or lard for frying

How to make:

1. Turn on oven. Set to Gas No. 4 —Electricity 350°.
2. Cut the crust from one long side of the sandwich loaf, then again from the long side cut a slice about 1 inch thick. Remove the surrounding crust from this slice.
3. Put a little oil or lard into the the frying pan and fry one side of the long slice of bread.
4. Place the bread, fried side down, on a 10 × 7 inch Swiss Roll tin or a baking tray.
5. Peel and chop the onions.
6. Skin 3 large tomatoes by plunging them quickly into boiling water.
7. Chop the tomatoes and add to the onions.
8. Put a little more oil or lard into the frying pan. Add the onions and tomatoes. Cover and cook gently for 20–25 minutes, until the mixture is soft and blended.
9. Drain the mixture and spread thickly on the bread in the tin.
10. Arrange the anchovy fillets, or spread paste, on top of the onion mixture.
11. Stone the olives, cut them in half and add them.
12. Bake in the centre of a moderate oven (Gas No. 4-Electricity 350°) for 15–20 minutes.
13. Serve in slices.

A sunny taste of the South of France.

2.

8.

9.

2.

3.

Salad Niçoise
(for 4 people)

French Dressing

1 dessertspoon wine vinegar
   or lemon juice
$\frac{1}{4}$ teaspoon mustard powder
1 teaspoon castor sugar
pinch of salt and pinch of black
   pepper
4 tablespoons olive oil
1 clove garlic (optional)

Salad

4 tomatoes
4 hard-boiled eggs
2 green peppers
2 small onions
1 can tuna fish
1 can anchovies
3 or 4 black olives

To make the French Dressing

1. Mix the wine vinegar or lemon juice with mustard powder, castor sugar, salt and black pepper.
2. Gradually add olive oil. Whisk well with a fork.
3. If using garlic, crush a clove with the blade of a knife and add the crushed clove to the dressing. Leave to stand while preparing the salad. Remove garlic before adding the dressing to the salad.

To make the salad

4. Cut the tomatoes and hard-boiled eggs roughly into quarters.
5. Remove stalks and seeds from the green peppers. Slice the skins finely.
6. Slice the onions as thinly as possible.
7. Combine all these ingredients in a salad bowl.
8. Drain and roughly flake the tuna fish. Add to salad.
9. Top with anchovies and olives.
10. Just before serving, remove garlic, if used, stir the French Dressing thoroughly and mix into the salad.

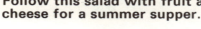

Follow this salad with fruit and cheese for a summer supper.

Indian Curry
(for 4—6 people)

You will need:

1 oz lard
4 onions
4 apples
2 tablespoons (approximately) curry powder
Up to 1 pint stock (or stock cubes and water)
3 oz sultanas
cooked meat, cooked chicken, cooked sausages or other leftovers
½ lemon

To serve with it

long-grain rice (4—6 portions)
mango chutney

Curry can be very hot. Adjust the amount of powder to suit your own taste.

How to make:

1. Melt the lard in a large saucepan.
2. Chop onions and add to hot fat.
3. Peel and core apples, chop and add. (Add more lard if necessary.)
4. Add 2 tablespoons curry powder (more if you like things hotter, less if you don't) and blend it in.
5. Add enough stock to cover. Blend thoroughly.
6. Add sultanas.
7. Chop the cooked meat, chicken, sausages or other left-overs and add.
8. Turn the heat down low, cover and allow to cook thoroughly (10—15 minutes).
9. Squeeze lemon over the curry before serving.
10. Serve with rice and mango chutney. Sliced tomatoes and cucumber with yoghurt are good with it too.

3.

7.

9.

1.

2.

3.

4.

Kedgeree
(for 4–6 people)

A breakfast and supper dish that originally came from India.

You will need:

¾ lb smoked cod or smoked haddock (without skin)
½ pint milk
3 eggs
6–8 oz long-grain rice
1 teaspoon salt
1½ pints cold water
4 oz butter
½ teaspoon ground black pepper

How to make:

1. Simmer the cod or haddock in the milk for 10 minutes. Drain and flake with a fork.
2. Bring a small pan of water to the boil, gently lower in the eggs and bring back to the boil. Boil for 10 minutes. Plunge eggs into cold water. When cool, remove the shells and chop roughly.
3. Into your largest pan put the rice, salt and cold water. Bring to the boil and simmer for 15 minutes (or until all the water is absorbed). Keep hot.
4. Mix the flaked fish and chopped eggs into the rice. Stir in the butter and black pepper.
   Reheat if necessary.
5. Serve immediately.

Cornish Pasties

(for 4 people)

Shortcrust Pastry

4 oz plain flour
pinch of salt
2 oz lard
1–2 tablespoons cold water
1 tablespoon milk

Filling

4 oz uncooked beef or lamb
1 large potato
1 large onion
salt and pepper

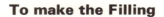

6.

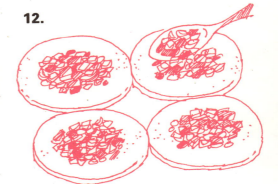

7.

To make Shortcrust Pastry

1. Turn on the oven. Set to Gas No. 6—Electricity 400°.
2. Sift flour and salt into a bowl.
3. Cut lard in small pieces. Rub into flour with your fingers.
4. When all the lard is evenly rubbed in, add 1 tablespoon cold water.
5. Mix round with your hand until you can lift out the 'dough' in one lump. If the mixture is too dry, add the second tablespoon water.
6. Sprinkle a little flour on the pastry board or table top and roll out the dough to an oblong about 10 × 12 inches.
7. Cut round a saucer to form three circles. Press the remaining pieces together, re-roll and cut fourth circle.

To make the Filling

8. Peel the potato and chop into small pieces.
9. Peel the onion and chop small.
10. Remove fat from meat and chop meat into small pieces.
11. Mix the potato, onion and meat. Add plenty of salt and pepper.
12. Divide the mixture into four. Place on the pastry circles.
13. Pinch up the edges to form a frill on top.
14. Place on a baking tray, brush with milk and bake near the top of a fairly hot oven (Gas No. 6—Electricity 400°) for 25–30 minutes.

12.

13.

Eat pasties either hot or cold.

A new way with sausages — from Germany.

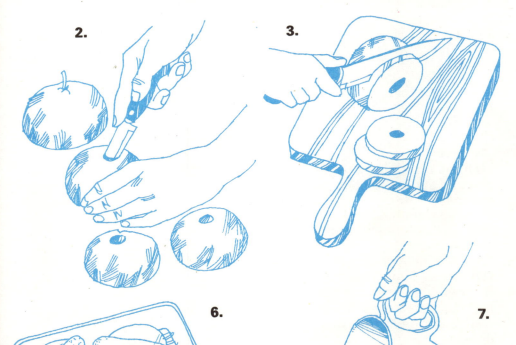

Sausages with Apple
(for 4—6 people)

You will need:

3—4 eating apples
butter or margarine
1 lb chipolata sausages
salt and pepper
$\frac{1}{2}$ pint stock (or cider if available)
mashed potato (4—6 portions)

How to make:

1. Turn on the oven. Set to Gas No. 6—Electricity 400°.
2. Core the apples with an apple corer, potato peeler or sharp knife, but do *not* peel them.
3. Slice them crosswise, into rings.
4. Grease a roasting tin with butter or margarine.
5. Lay the apple rings in the roasting tin.
6. Put the sausages on the apples.
7. Season and pour over hot stock or cider.
8. Bake in a fairly hot oven (Gas No. 6—Electricity 400°) for approximately 1 hour, turning the sausages at least once, until the apple is soft and the sausages are pale brown all over.
9. Serve on a bed of hot mashed potato.

Moussaka
(for 6 people)

Moussaka is a traditional dish from Greece.

You will need:

4 aubergines (egg plant)
2 large onions
cooking oil
1 lb minced beef
salt and pepper
1 small can of tomatoes
$\frac{1}{4}$ pint beef stock (made with a stock cube)
2 tablespoons flour seasoned with salt and pepper
black olives (if available)

Cheese Sauce

6 oz grated cheese (Cheddar and Parmesan mixed)
1 oz margarine
1 oz flour
$\frac{1}{2}$ pint milk

How to make:

1. Turn on the oven. Set to Gas No. 4—Electricity 350°.
2. Have ready an ovenproof dish.
3. Slice the aubergines and sprinkle with salt to remove the bitterness. Leave aside.
4. Chop the onions roughly and fry in the oil.
5. Add the meat, taking care to break it up as it cooks. Season with salt and pepper.
6. Add tomatoes and stock.
7. Allow to simmer, stirring occasionally, until the meat is browned. Set aside.
   Clean the frying pan and add a little more oil.
8. Pat the sliced aubergines dry with kitchen paper. Dip in seasoned flour.
9. Fry in the oil until soft.
10. In an ovenproof dish lay first a layer of aubergines, then a layer of meat alternately until there are three layers of aubergines and two of meat.

How to make:

11. Melt the margarine in a small pan and stir in the flour. Cook for one minute.
12. Remove from heat and add milk gradually, stirring to avoid lumps.
13. Return to heat and cook, stirring, for 3 minutes.
14. Remove from heat and add half the grated cheese. Stir well. Season with salt and pepper.
15. Pour the cheese sauce over the meat and aubergines.
16. Sprinkle the remaining cheese on top.
17. Halve the olives (if used). Remove the stones and arrange, cut-side-down, to decorate the top.
18. Bake in a moderate oven (Gas No. 4—Electricity 350°) for 20—25 minutes.
19. Before serving, remove excess oil with a spoon, or 'blot' with kitchen paper if necessary.

10.

15.

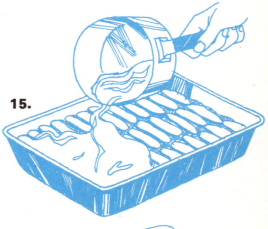

17.

Buck Rarebit
(for 4 people)

You will need:

8 oz Cheddar cheese
6 tablespoons milk
pinch of dry mustard
pinch of cayenne pepper
1 teaspoon Worcester sauce
5 eggs
4 small slices of toast (trimmed)

How to make:

1. Grate the cheese into a pan.
2. Melt it over a very low heat.
3. As the cheese begins to melt gradually stir in the milk.
4. Add the mustard, cayenne and Worcester sauce and stir thoroughly.
5. Break I egg into a bowl, beat and add to the cheese mixture in the pan.
6. Stir until thick and creamy. Remove from heat and keep warm.
7. Poach four eggs.
8. Pour the Rarebit over the pieces of toast, top each one with an egg and serve immediately.

A tasty variation on Welsh Rarebit.

Spaghetti al Burro
(for 4–6 people)

You will need:

2 pints water
1 teaspoon salt
1 lb spaghetti
4 oz butter
6 tablespoons grated cheese
(Parmesan if possible)
pepper (black if available) for
seasoning

How to make:

1. Bring the water to the boil, add salt.
2. Hold the spaghetti in one hand and slide it into the water. It will soften as it cooks.
3. Boil for 12 minutes. Drain.
4. Stir in butter and 4 tablespoons of the grated cheese. Sprinkle liberally with pepper.
5. Serve very hot, sprinkled with remaining cheese.

Italians hold their forks upright, prongs down, in spaghetti and twist to get a forkful. If you find this difficult, give up and use a spoon!

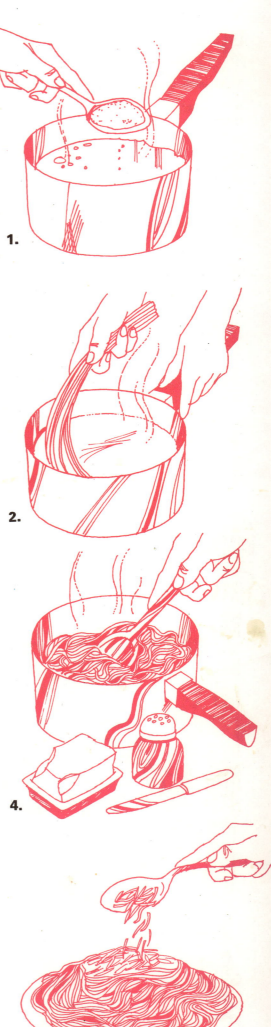

1.

2.

4.

5.

Lasagne
(for 4—6 people)

You will need:

2 pints water
1 teaspoon salt
6 oz lasagne

Bolognese Sauce

2 onions
2 tablespoons cooking oil
   or 2 oz lard
8 oz minced beef
salt, pepper, herbs (if available)
1 small (2¼ oz) can of
   tomato purée
¼ pint stock or water

Cheese Sauce

6 oz cheese
1 oz margarine
1 oz flour
½ pint milk

Serve this meat sauce with spaghetti to make Spaghetti Bolognese, as shown opposite.

To cook the Lasagne

1. Put the water, with salt, into a large pan and bring to the boil. Add the lasagne, pushing it in with a wooden spoon as it softens. Boil for 12 minutes, then remove from heat, drain, rinse in cold water and leave aside.

To make Bolognese Sauce

2. Chop onions.
3. Heat cooking oil or lard in a saucepan and fry the chopped onion until transparent (about 5 minutes).
4. Add the minced beef, and cook, stirring constantly, until brown.
5. Season with salt and pepper and add a sprinkling of herbs if available.
6. Pour off any excess fat.
7. Add tomato purée and stock or water.
8. Simmer gently for 20 minutes.
9. Turn on the oven. Set to Gas No. 7—Electricity 425°.

To make the Cheese Sauce

10. Grate the cheese (or mix grated Cheddar and Parmesan).
11. Melt the margarine and stir in the flour. Cook for one minute. Remove from heat and add milk gradually, stirring to avoid lumps. Return to heat and cook, stirring, for 3 minutes.
12. Remove from heat and add half the cheese. Stir well. Season with salt and pepper.
13. Grease an ovenproof dish and cover the bottom with lasagne.
14. Cover thinly with Bolognese sauce, then with cheese sauce.
15. Add a second layer of lasagne and again cover with Bolognese sauce and then with cheese sauce. Continue until all the sauce is used.
16. Top with a layer of lasagne and sprinkle on the remaining grated cheese.
17. Bake near the top of a hot oven (Gas No. 7—Electricity 425°) for 20—25 minutes.

If you cannot toss pancakes turn them with a palette knife or fish-slice.

5.

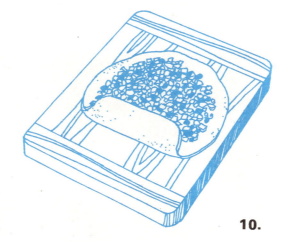

10.

11.

Savoury Pancakes
(for 4–6 people)

You will need:

4 oz flour
2 eggs
1 tablespoon cooking oil
8 tablespoons milk
2 tablespoons water
pinch of salt

Filling

8 oz of either cooked chicken, meat, sausages or vegetables.
1 oz margarine
1 oz flour
12 tablespoons ($\frac{1}{4} + \frac{1}{8}$ pint) milk
As for *Moussaka* (see page 30).

How to make:

1. Grease a frying pan with oil or lard.
2. Sift the flour into a bowl. Break the eggs into the centre. Add cooking oil and milk. Beat very thoroughly.
3. Add 1 tablespoon water and beat again.
4. Fry a small 'test' pancake. If the mixture flows too stiffly to form a thin pancake, add another tablespoon of water.
5. Fill a saucepan with hot water, put it on the stove and cover with an upturned plate. Put the cooked pancakes over the plate to keep warm.
6. Make the pancakes thin, frying until just set and lightly browned on each side.

To make the Filling

7. Chop the chicken. Season. Add any other chopped left-overs such as sausages, potato or vegetables.
8. In a small pan, melt the margarine, stir in the flour to form a 'roux', remove from the heat and stir in 8 tablespoons milk. Re-heat and stir until smooth. Stir in 4 further tablespoons milk over the heat. Cook for a further two minutes.
9. Add the chicken and other filling ingredients. Stir and heat through.
10. Lay each pancake flat, fill with filling and roll up.
11. If liked, serve with a *Cheese Sauce* (as used for *Moussaka*, see page 30).

Scotch Eggs

(for 4 people)

You will need:

Oil for deep frying
5 eggs
4 sausages
crisp breadcrumbs

How to make:

1. Half fill a saucepan with cooking oil. Fit a frying basket into the pan and leave aside.
2. Bring a pan of water to the boil, put in 4 eggs, bring back to the boil and boil for 10 minutes. Remove, plunge eggs into cold water and remove shells.
3. Skin the sausages and cover each egg with the meat from one sausage, being careful to leave no cracks.
4. Break one egg into a deep plate and mix the yolk and white with a fork. Into a second deep plate put about 2 tablespoons crisp breadcrumbs.
5. Roll the eggs covered with sausagemeat, first in the egg, then in the breadcrumbs, until completely covered.
6. Heat the oil in the saucepan, still with the frying basket in place, until a square of bread thrown into it browns and rises to the top. *Ask a grown-up to help with deep-frying. Hot fat is dangerous.*
7. Put the four eggs into the basket and lower it into the fat. Cook until golden brown (2–3 minutes).
8. Remove, cut each Scotch Egg in two and serve hot with mashed potato and peas.

Scotch Eggs can also be eaten cold — they are specially good for picnics.

3.

5.

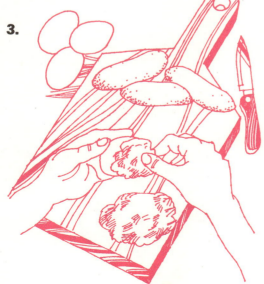

7.

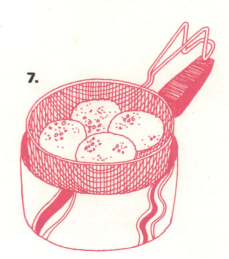

Cheese Fondue
(for 4—6 people)

You will need:

1 lb Cheddar cheese
4 tablespoons dry cider
½ teaspoon Worcester sauce
pinch of salt
pinch of cayenne pepper
French bread
radishes, cauliflower-sprigs, carrot
 sticks, celery

How to make:

1. Grate the cheese into a pan or
   a flameproof dish.
2. Stir over a gentle heat until
   it melts.
3. Gradually add cider and
   Worcester sauce. Stir
   thoroughly.
4. Season with salt and cayenne
   pepper.
5. Cut French bread into 1-inch
   cubes.
6. Wash and cut up vegetables.
7. Keep warm and serve as a party
   dip with cubes of French
   bread, radishes, raw cauliflower
   sprigs and raw carrot and
   celery cut in sticks.

**This English version of a Swiss
favourite is perfect for a party.**

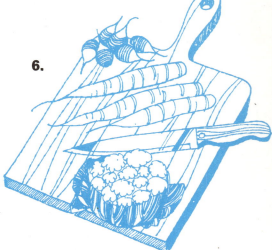

Cheese Soufflé
(for 4–6 people)

You will need:

$1\frac{1}{2}$ oz margarine
$1\frac{1}{2}$ oz plain flour
$\frac{1}{2}$ teaspoon mixed mustard
$\frac{1}{2}$ teaspoon salt
pinch of cayenne pepper
$\frac{1}{3}$ pint milk (approx. 1 teacup)
3 oz grated Cheddar cheese
+1 oz grated Parmesan *or* 4 oz
   grated Cheddar
4 eggs (3 eggs +1 white)

How to make:

1. Turn on the oven. Set to Gas No. 4—Electricity 350°.
2. Have ready a 2 pint (8 inch) soufflé dish.
3. Melt the margarine in a pan over low heat, stir in the flour, mustard, salt and cayenne.
4. Remove from heat and add the milk gradually, stirring all the time.
5. Return to heat and boil for three minutes, stirring.
6. Add the cheese and continue stirring until melted. Remove from heat.
7. Separate the egg yolks from the whites. Put the yolks of

9.

10.

11.

three eggs into a bowl and beat.
(Cover the fourth yolk with water and keep in the refrigerator.)
8. Add the beaten yolks to the mixture in the pan. Mix well.
9. Beat the four egg whites until stiff.
10. Pour the cheese mixture on to the whites. Fold together thoroughly.
11. Pour into the soufflé dish (ungreased) and bake in a moderate oven (Gas No. 4—Electricity 350°) for 35–40 minutes. *Serve at once.*

Never keep a soufflé waiting – it must be served at once.

Herbs & Vegetables

Next time you pass the greengrocer's, look out for some of these unusual herbs and vegetables. Always ask if you see something you do not recognise. The greengrocer can advise you how to cook it too.

Globe artichoke

Boil in salted water for about 30 minutes. Serve with melted butter, as a first course or main dish.

Jerusalem artichoke

Peel and boil in salted water. Serve in a white sauce with meat or fish. Make into purée for an excellent soup.

Savoy

Cabbage. Shred and boil in a little salted water with caraway seeds. Toss in butter or margarine. Serve with meat.

Chicory

Use raw in salads or braise in the oven with a very little water, butter and salt. In some countries chicory is known as *endive*.

Parsnips

Peel and remove hard core. Slice and boil. Toss in melted margarine and serve with meat.

Tomatoes

Halve, sprinkle with basil or mixed dried herbs, top with a knob of butter and grill; or cut a zig-zag around the centre and use to garnish a salad.

Courgettes

Baby marrows, also called *zucchini*. Boil; or slice, flour and fry.

Green peppers

Remove seeds, slice and add to salad; or stuff with a savoury mince mixture and bake.

Aubergines

Slice and fry, or stuff with onion and tomato and bake. Use in *Moussaka.* Aubergines are also known as egg plant.

Fennel

Tastes of aniseed. Slice for salads. Slice and stew to serve with fish or chicken.

Endive

Use instead of lettuce. Known as *chicory* in some countries including France and U.S.A.

Radishes

Wash and top and tail. Cut a cross or star down to base (but not right through) and put in cold water to open into 'roses'. Use to garnish salads.

Cucumber

Draw a fork down the skin then slice thinly into 'cogwheels'. Use to garnish fish and cold meat.

Garlic

Crush one clove and add to stews. Remove before serving. Very strong, so never use too much.

Chives

Chop and add to salad, soups or stews.

Bay

Add one leaf to sauces, soups and stews. Remove before serving.

Mint

Boil with new peas or new potatoes. Remove before serving.

Rosemary

Lay over roast lamb while it is cooking. Remove before serving.

Basil

A herb to sprinkle over tomatoes or in stews.

Lemon

Rub a cut lemon over chicken or turkey before roasting to give a lovely crisp brown skin.

Cayenne

A finely ground red pepper. Very hot so use sparingly.

Vegetables are best when they are crisp or firm.

Desserts

After the main course, serve one of these delicious desserts. Offer people small helpings first, saving some for seconds. You could eat Cheesecake or Lemon Sorbet at tea-time too.

3.

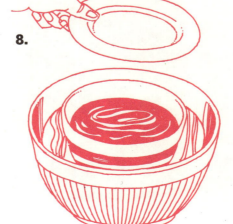

8.

This is a simple version of a classic French dessert.

Nègre en Chemise
(for 4–6 people)

You will need:
4½ tablespoons cornflour
1½ tablespoons cocoa
4 tablespoons sugar
1 pint milk
1 tablespoon coffee essence

Sweet White Sauce

2 oz butter or margarine
1½ tablespoons flour
2 tablespoons sugar
½ pint milk
few drops of vanilla

How to make:

1. Sift together the cornflour, cocoa and sugar.
2. Mix with approximately ¼ pint milk. Add coffee essence. Stir thoroughly to remove lumps.
3. Bring the rest of the milk to the boil and pour half of this on to the cornflour mixture, stirring all the time.
4. Return cornflour mixture to the remaining milk in pan.
5. Bring to the boil. Boil, stirring, for 3 minutes.
6. Pour into a bowl, previously rinsed out with cold water.
7. Cover with a plate to prevent a 'skin' forming.
8. Stand in a larger bowl, part filled with cold water to cool and set.

To make Sweet White Sauce

9. Melt 1 oz butter or margarine. Remove from heat.
10. Blend in flour and sugar.
11. Add milk and vanilla, and blend thoroughly.
12. Return to heat and stir until boiling. Boil for 3 minutes.
13. Remove from heat. Stir in remaining 1 oz butter and allow to cool.
14. Stir before serving.
15. When cold, turn the chocolate out of the mould on to a dish. Cover with sweet white sauce.

11.

American Cheesecake
(for 4–6 people)

You will need:

6 oz digestive (wheatmeal) biscuits (about 12)
3 oz butter
3 eggs (2 eggs and 1 white)
1 lb curd cheese (or processed cream cheese)
5 oz castor sugar
½ teaspoon vanilla essence
2 oz sultanas

How to make:

1. Turn on the oven. Set to Gas No. 6—Electricity 400°.
2. Put the biscuits into a plastic bag and crush them with a rolling pin. Put the crumbs into a bowl.
3. Butter the bottom and sides of a 7 inch cake tin with a removable base.
4. Melt the butter and pour on to the biscuit crumbs. Mix well.
5. Press the crumb and butter mixture into the bottom of the cake tin and about 2 inches up the sides to form a shell for the cheesecake.
6. Bake in a fairly hot oven (Gas No. 6—Electricity 400°) for 10 minutes, take out of the oven and leave in the cake tin to cool.
7. Turn down the oven to Gas No. 4—Electricity 350°.
8. Separate the eggs, putting *two* yolks into one bowl and *three* whites into another. (Cover the third yolk with water and keep in the refrigerator until wanted).
9. Add the cheese, sugar and vanilla essence to the egg yolks and mix, beating until all lumps have disappeared.
10. Beat the egg whites until stiff, then blend into the cheese mixture.
11. Clean the sultanas by sifting them with a tablespoon of flour. Stir the sultanas into the mixture.
12. Pour the mixture on to the biscuit base and bake in a moderate oven (Gas No. 4—Electricity 350°) for 35—40 minutes, until the top is firm and pale brown.
13. Cool in the cake tin. When quite cold remove the tin and serve on the removable base.
14. Serve in *small* slices as this cheesecake is deliciously rich.

2.

5.

12.

13.

There is plenty of Cheesecake here for second helpings!

Apple Dumplings

(for 4–6 people)

Shortcrust Pastry

8 oz plain flour
pinch of salt
4 oz lard and margarine mixed
3–4 tablespoons cold water

Filling

4 large or 6 small sweet apples
1 oz dried fruit
1 oz demerara or soft brown sugar
2 tablespoons milk

To make Shortcrust Pastry

1. Turn on the oven. Set to Gas No. 8—Electricity 450°.
2. Sift the flour with a pinch of salt into a mixing bowl.
3. Cut the lard and margarine into small pieces and rub into the flour with the fingertips.
4. When all the fat is evenly rubbed in, add 3 tablespoons cold water and mix with the hand until you can lift the 'dough' out in one lump. If the mixture is too dry, add the fourth tablespoon of water.
5. Sprinkle a little flour on the pastry board or table top and roll out the dough to a large square or circle.

To make Dumplings

6. Peel and core the apples.
7. Place each apple in turn on the pastry and cut a large circle round it.
8. Mix the dried fruit and brown sugar. With a teaspoon, fill the hole left by the core of each apple with this mixture.
9. Fold the pastry up round each apple to cover it completely.
10. Turn the apples upside down on the baking tray so that the 'seams' are underneath.
11. From the leftover pastry cut two large 'leaves' for each dumpling. Mark the 'veins' with the back of a knife. Cut a thin strip of dough and roll up to form the stalk and place a stalk and leaves on each apple dumpling. Brush with milk.
12. Bake in a very hot oven (Gas No. 8—Electricity 450°) for 10–12 minutes, until the pastry is just turning colour.
13. Lower the oven to moderate (Gas No. 4—Electricity 350°) continue baking for a further 20–25 minutes for the apples to cook through.
Serve hot.

Dumplings are very filling so serve after a light main course.

3.

9.

12.

Lemon Sorbet
(for 4–6 people)

If you have ice lolly moulds use this recipe, without the egg, to make your own ice lollies.

You will need:

3 lemons
6 oz loaf sugar
1 pint cold water
1 small egg

How to make:

1. Fill a 7 × 4 inch loaf tin with cold water and leave aside.
2. Peel the lemons very thinly, with a potato peeler or sharp knife.
3. Squeeze the juice out of the peeled lemons.
4. Put the rind into a pan with the sugar and water.
5. Heat gently to dissolve the sugar, then bring to the boil and boil *fast* for 6 minutes.
6. Remove from heat and stand pan in cold water to cool.
7. Separate the white from the yolk of the egg. Beat the white until stiff.
8. Add the lemon juice to the sugar mixture in the pan.

9. When cool, strain (to remove the rind) straight on to the white of egg.
10. Fold them together with a metal spoon. (If some of the white persists in rising to the top, don't worry—it will taste good and look pretty when frozen.)
11. Empty the loaf tin and pour the lemon mixture into the undried tin.
12. Set in the ice-making compartment of the refrigerator overnight.
13. If you want it sooner, turn the refrigerator to MAX, remembering to remove foods you do not want turned to ice!

Sweets

Everyone in the family will enjoy helping you make these sweets — and they will enjoy eating them too. Wrap some in greaseproof and gift wrapping to give as little party prizes or presents.

Use peppermint essence and green colouring, instead of vanilla and cochineal, to make Crème de Menthe.

Turkish Delight

You will need:

¾ pint cold water
1 lb granulated sugar
1 oz (2 × ½ oz packets) powdered gelatine
few drops of vanilla or other essence
few drops of cochineal or other colouring
1 oz cornflour
1 oz icing sugar

How to make:

1. Fill a 7 × 7 inch square tin with cold water and leave aside.
2. Put ¼ pint of cold water and the granulated sugar in a pan and dissolve the sugar, stirring occasionally, over a low heat.
3. Put ½ pint cold water and the powdered gelatine into your largest saucepan and dissolve over a low heat.
4. When both the sugar and the gelatine are wholly dissolved, pour the sugar mixture into the pan containing the gelatine and mix.
5. Add the flavouring and colouring , bring to the boil, and boil *fast* for 20 minutes. Remove from heat and cool by standing the pan in cold water until it resembles liquid jelly. *It must not set at all.*
6. Empty the water from the tin and pour the Turkish Delight into the undried tin.
7. Leave overnight to set.
8. Sift the cornflour and icing sugar together.
9. Have ready a pan of hot water and a knife. Cut gently round the edge of the tin, warming the knife in the hot water when it sticks. Then, still warming the knife, cut the Turkish Delight into long strips about 1 inch wide. Toss the strips in the cornflour and sugar mixture, cut them into squares and toss again. Serve as a sweet or with coffee after a meal.

(Makes approximately 1 lb 6 oz)

Vanilla Fudge

You will need:

½ lb granulated sugar
2 tablespoons water
1 oz butter
6 tablespoons full cream
   sweetened condensed milk
few drops vanilla essence

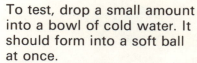

How to make:

1. Butter the bottom and sides of a 7 × 4 inch loaf tin (or a metal ice-tray from the refrigerator).
2. Put the sugar, water and butter together into a large saucepan and heat gently, stirring until the sugar is dissolved, when there should be no more 'gritty' feeling at the bottom of the pan.
3. Add the condensed milk and mix thoroughly.
   Bring to the boil and boil to the 'soft ball' stage (240°F if using a sugar thermometer).

To test, drop a small amount into a bowl of cold water. It should form into a soft ball at once.

4. When this stage is reached, remove pan from heat and add vanilla essence.
5. Beat mixture until it begins to thicken and reaches the consistency of thick treacle. *It must not be too thick to pour.*
6. Pour into the prepared tin and leave until hard.
7. When hard, cut into squares with a sharp knife.

(Makes approximately 10 oz)

5.

7.

Store sweets
in air-tight
jars or tins.

Peanut Brittle

You will need:

4 oz roasted peanuts
8 oz sugar
4 tablespoons water
squeeze of lemon juice

How to make:

1. Butter a 7 inch square tin.
2. Chop the peanuts.
3. Dissolve the sugar in the water in a large saucepan over a low heat. Add the lemon juice.
4. Bring gently to the boil.
5. As the sugar begins to turn colour, remove from the heat, add the chopped peanuts and pour into the prepared tin. Do not let the sugar turn too brown. *It must not burn.*
6. When set, break into bite-sized pieces.
   (Makes approximately ¾ lb)

5.

INSTRUCTIONS

FOR

TRAVELLERS

1757

JOSIAH TUCKER

RE-ISSUED IN A SERIES OF REPRINTS OF
CLASSIC ENGLISH WORKS ON
THE HISTORY AND DEVELOPMENT OF
ECONOMIC THOUGHT,
UNDER THE EDITORIAL DIRECTION OF
PROFESSOR W. E. MINCHINTON
UNIVERSITY OF EXETER

S. R. PUBLISHERS LIMITED
JOHNSON REPRINT CORPORATION

This reproduction has been made with the kind permission of the Goldsmiths' Librarian, University of London, from the copy held in the Goldsmiths' Library, Senate House, London, W.C. 1.

The publishers would like to acknowledge the assistance of Dr. J. H. P. Pafford, M.A., F.S.A., F.L.A., the former Goldsmiths' Librarian, Miss M. B. C. Canney of the Goldsmiths' Library and Mr. F. J. Bosley, M.I.R.T., the chief photographer to the Goldsmiths' Library, without whose assistance this series of reprints could not have been successfully undertaken.

Library of Congress Catalog Card Number: 73-114071

British Standard Book Number: 85409-257-9

S. R. Publishers Ltd.
East Ardsley, Wakefield
Yorkshire, England

Johnson Reprint Corporation
111 Fifth Avenue
New York, N.Y. 10003, U.S.A.

Printed in the U.S.A.

INSTRUCTIONS

FOR

TRAVELLERS.

1757.

ADVERTISEMENT.

THE *following Pages are a Part of the Work, which the Author of* The Elements of Commerce, and Theory of Taxes, *propofed to offer to public Confideration. The Subject of them is of great Importance, though not the next in order according to the original Plan.* This Alteration is owing to the Requeft, or rather Command (for fuch it ought to be efteemed) of a Perfon equally eminent for his great Learning and Public Spirit, as for his Rank and Quality; who being advanced beyond the ufual Age of Man, was defirous of feeing the INSTRUCTIONS FOR TRAVELLERS before the Reft of the Work could be completed. And as the general Plan will receive a particular Illuftration by it, the Author humbly hopes, That this Anticipation will not be difagreeable to the Reft of his worthy Friends. The Breadth of the Margin is the fame with the former: And the Prefs is ftill to be confidered only as a more expeditious Amanuenfis. Due Thanks are returned by the Author for the Corrections and Amendments already received; and he earneftly folicits the Continuance and Increafe of thefe Favours.

A PLAN *for improving in the moral and political Theory of Trade and Taxes, by means of Travelling.*

PERSONS who propofe to themfelves a Scheme for Travelling, generally do it with a View to obtain one, or more of the following Ends, *viz. Firſt*, To make curious Collections as Natural Philofophers, Virtuofos, or Antiquarians. *Secondly*, To improve in Painting, Statuary, Architecture, and Mufic. *Thirdly*, To obtain the Reputation of being Men of Vertù, and of an elegant Tafte. *Fourthly*, To acquire foreign Airs, and adorn their dear Perfons with fine Cloaths and new Fafhions, and their Converfation with new Phrafes. Or, *Fifthly*, To rub off local Prejudices (which is indeed the moſt commendable Motive, though not the moſt prevailing) and to acquire that enlarged and impartial View of Men and Things, which no one fingle Country can afford. — Thefe, I fay, are the principal Inducements for modern Travelling : Though it muſt be owned, that there is one particular Clafs of Travellers yet to mention, whofe Motives are very fingular, and their Number very fmall; thofe, I mean, who refolve to vifit the Countries of *Italy* and *Greece*, out of a Kind of enthufiaſtic Reverence for Claffic Ground, like the Pilgrims of old for the Holy Land, and paying a Sort of Literary Adoration to the very Rubbifh of an antient City, or to any Spot of Earth that has been famous in antient Story. [As to that Species of Beings found only here in *England* (a Country of univerfal Freedom and Opulence) who go Abroad with no other Views but becaufe they are tired of ſtaying at Home, and can afford to make themfelves as ridiculous every where as they pleafe : It would be Lofs of Time to take any other Notice of them, than juſt to obferve, That they are fure of returning Home as Wife as they went out, but much more Impertinent, lefs Wealthy, and lefs Innocent.]

Now, though the Scheme to be propofed in the following Pages, is not immediately calculated for the Ufe of either of the Clafſes of Travellers abovementioned, yet the Author is humbly of Opinion, that all might perufe it without Difadvantage, if not with fome Degree of Improvement.   But ſtill the Perſon, for whom this Plan is particularly intended, muſt be a Man whoſe Views in Travelling are of a different Nature from either of the former : That is, he muſt make thoſe Things in which their Buſineſs and Imployment chiefly conſiſted, to be only his Amuſement and occaſional Recreations ; and muſt dedicate his principal Studies towards tracing ſuch ſecret, tho' powerful Effects and Conſequences, as are produced by the various Syſtems of Religion, Government, and Commerce in the World: He muſt obſerve, how theſe Syſtems operate on different People, or on the ſame People in different Periods, *viz.* Whether they enlarge, or contract the active Powers in human Nature, and whether they make thoſe Powers become uſeful, or pernicious to Society.   For in Fact, the human mind is in ſome Senſe but as Clay in the Hands of the Potter, which receives its Figure and Impreſſion, if I may ſo ſpeak, according as it is moulded or formed by theſe different Syſtems : So that the Political, the Religious, and Commercial Characters of any People will be found for the moſt Part to be the Reſult of this three-fold Combination of Religion, Government, and Commerce on their Minds.   Now Travelling into foreign Countries for the Sake of Improvement, neceſſarily pre-ſuppoſes, that you are no Stranger to the Religion, Conſtitution, and Nature of your own.   For if you go abroad before you have laid in a competent Stock of this Sort of Knowledge, how can you make uſeful Compariſons between your own and other Countries ?   How can you judge concerning the Preference which ought to be given either to the one, or the other ? Or ſelect thoſe Things from Abroad, which may with Advantage be naturalized at Home ?   Therefore let a young Gentleman begin with the Tour of his Country, under the Guidance of a ſkilful Inſtructor : Let him examine the general Properties of the Soil, the Climate, and the like :   And attend to the Characteriſtics of the Inhabitants, and the Nature of the ſeveral Eſtabliſhments, Religious, Civil, Military, and Commercial.   And then, and not till then, is he completely Qualified to make Obſervations on foreign Countries.

But in order to proceed even thus far, a young Gentleman ſhould not only have paſſed through the common Forms of a liberal Education, but alſo ſhould have attentively peruſed ſuch particular Treatiſes, as might beſt ſerve to inſtruct him in the Buſineſs he is to ſet about, and to anſwer the Purpoſes here propoſed : For an ignorant Traveller is of all Beings the moſt contemptible : And the beſt that you can ſay of him is, that he ſees ſtrange Sights in ſtrange Coun-

tries

tries with the ſame ſtupid, wondering Face of Praiſe, which the common People do Feats of Juggling and Legerdemain at Home. Beſides, if a young Perſon is not ſufficiently grounded in right Principles before he ſets out, it will be ſeldom in his Power, and ſeldomer ſtill in his Inclination, to acquire them afterwards; eſpecially during his Travels. For Travelling is by no means the proper Seaſon for acquiring the Rudiments of Knowledge, but for making a judicious Application of former Acquirements.

THEREFORE the Author humbly hopes, that the candid and judicious Reader will forgive him in his well-meant Endeavours in recommending a few Books to the Peruſal and Study of the young Pupil before ſetting out: And in adding ſhort Obſervations upon them.

Religion. } *Seed*'s Sermons, two firſt vol. *Sherlock*'s Sermons, three vol. Biſhop of *Sodor and Man*'s Inſtructions for *Indians*.

Ethics, Civil Law, and Government in general. } *Burlamachi*'s Natural and Political Law; *Burnet*'s Eſſay on Government; *Monteſquieu*'s L'Eſprit de Loix.

Peculiar Syſtem of the *Engliſh* Conſtitution. } *Rapin*'s Diſſertation on the Government of the *Anglo-Saxons*, and his Diſſertation on Whig and Tory; *Monteſquieu*'s Chapters on the *Engliſh* Conſtitution, *viz.* Book XI. Chap. 6. and Book XIX. Chap. 27. The Analyſis of the Laws of *England*; alſo the preſent State of *England*.

Eſtabliſhment of the Church of *England*, and a Toleration. } *Warburton*'s Alliance between Church and State.

Foreign Politics, and Balance of Power. } *Campbell*'s Preſent State of *Europe*.

Commerce, and Taxes. } Sir *Joſiah Child* on Trade; Remarks on the Advantages, and Diſadvantages of *France*, and *Great Britain*; *Crouche*'s Book of Rates.

OBSERVATIONS.

I. WE muſt firſt begin with Religion, not only becauſe it is the moſt Important in its Nature, but becauſe if a Traveller is not well

grounded

grounded in the Principles of it before he ſets out, he will run the Riſk either of having none at all during his whole Life, or of being made a Convert to a very bad one, I mean the Popiſh. For if his Turn of Mind is naturally Contemplative and Philoſophic, the great Variety of Religions he will meet with in his Travels will ſo ſtagger his Reſolution as to make him indifferent to all alike; at the ſame Time, that the impudent Tricks and Forgeries of the Church of *Rome*, will tempt him to pronounce the Whole a Cheat. But if he ſhould have any ſtrong Tincture of Enthuſiaſm, or Superſtition in his Compoſition; or if he ſhould be pre-diſpoſed either to an Exceſs of Gaiety, or of Gloom, or be captivated with outſide Forms, at the ſame Time that he went on in a Round of thoughtleſs Pleaſure; in all theſe Reſpects the Religion of the Church of *Rome* is particularly calculated for making Proſelytes of young Minds, by applying her Snares, either to this Foible, or to that, according to the predominant Diſpoſition. Therefore in every View, and upon every Account, it ought to be laid down as an indiſputable Maxim, that a young Gentleman ought not to begin his Travels, while he is a Novice in the important Concerns of Religion.

Now the firſt Book recommended is *Seed*'s Sermons, which having the Advantage of a great Luxuriancy and Brilliancy of Stile, are fitter to make their Way into the Hearts of young People, than Authors more exact in their Compoſition, and of a leſs flowery Imagination. But there is beſide this, a very peculiar Reaſon for recommending theſe Diſcourſes, and that is, that as their Reaſoning is, for the moſt Part, grounded on Biſhop *Butler*'s *Analogy*, they exhibit in the gayeſt and moſt inviting Colours, the Strength, and Chain of Thought of that deep, ſagacious Author, without his metaphyſical Stile, or abſtract Speculations. As to Biſhop *Butler* himſelf, he certainly purſues a Method the fitteſt in the World to put to ſilence the ſuperficial, licentious Extravagancies of modern Times; were his manner of Writing a little more pleaſing and alluring. For by demonſtrating, that there is a Syſtem actually carrying on by the Author of the Univerſe, both in the natural and moral World, he confutes the Sceptics on one Extreme; and by proving how imperfectly this Syſtem is yet comprehended by us, he checks that Arrogance, and Self-ſufficiency on the other, which are too natural to young Minds, juſt tinctured with a Smattering of Knowledge. As to Biſhop *Sherlock*'s Sermons, whether you conſider the Author as the diſtinguiſhed Defender of the ſublime Truths of Religion, or as throwing

new

new and unexpected Lights on old and common Subjects, or as a fagacious Textuarift, a found practical Writer, a judicious Cafuift, or an eminent Model of clear, nervous, and manly Eloquence:—In all thefe Refpects he is great without a Rival. And no Man, whatever his future Profeffion in Life is intended to be, would mifemploy his Time in giving him a careful and attentive Perufal. In regard to the Bifhop of *Sodor and Man's Inftructions for the* Indians, it is enough to fay, that it is the beft Compendium of practical Divinity yet extant. And as a Gentleman ought to carry fome little Tract or other with him Abroad both for Reading, and Devotion (for I dare not fuppofe that the Life of a Traveller will be the Life of an Atheift) he cannot carry a fitter Author into foreign Countries than this here recommended; an Author, who by happily felecting the more effential and fundamental Truths of Religion, from others of lefs Importance, hath kept clear of all Controverfy, and wrote in fuch a manner as to be acceptable to the Members of every Chriftian Communion whatever.

Note, This Author is tranflated into *French*.

II. NEXT to Religion, and indeed as a Part thereof, though too frequently confidered in a different View, are Ethics, Civil Law, and the Rudiments of Government in general. In which Cafe *Burlamachi*'s two Treatifes contain all the Inftructions neceffary for a young Gentleman juft fetting out upon his Travels: It being the great Happinefs of this Author to exprefs himfelf in very clear and intelligible Terms upon the abftrufeft Subjects, and to reconcile the feemingly contradictory Opinions and Syftems of thofe who wrote before him, by unravelling the Meaning of each, and fhewing, that the chief Difference between them was a Difference of Expreffion. By thefe Means he hath fixed the Science of Legiflation, if I may fo fpeak, by clear and determinate Rules; and hath laid a firm Foundation for future Legiflators to build upon; I fay, *future* Legiflators; becaufe in a Conftitution fuch as ours, it is not at all improbable, but the young Gentleman Traveller will one Day come to have a Share in making Laws for the Good of his Country: And therefore he ought certainly to know fomething of the Nature of them. In regard to Dr *Burnet's Effay on Government*, as it is written with peculiar Clearnefs and Precifion, and proceeds in a mathematic or fcientific Way; it has undoubtedly great Merit; and being fo very fhort and compendious, it will take up but little Time in Reading. *The Spirit of Laws* of Monfieur *de Montefquieu* is fuperior to all Elogiums whatever.

III. AFTER

III. AFTER an Acquisition of the Rudiments of Ethics and Civil Law, and some Insight into the general Nature of Government, it will be highly requisite to enter into the peculiar Spirit of the *British* Constitution. To which End, *Rapin's Dissertation on the Government of the* Anglo-Saxons, and his *Dissertation on Whigs and Tories*, will be highly useful, both as they give a general Idea of the antient Gothic Plan, which is the Basis of the present, and as they point out those great and important Revolutions which have since ensued: So that by comparing both together, a judicious Reader may be the more able to form an exact Idea of the Benefits or Dangers proceeding either from the former, or the latter Constitution. But as to the modern Spirit of our Government, its Guards, Limits, and Correctives, perhaps no Author can equal the Baron *de Montesquieu* in his Chapters on the *English* Constitution, Book XI. Chap. 6. Book XIX. Chap. 27. Note also, that before a young Gentleman actually sets out to visit foreign Countries, he ought to have received a few Lectures on the Nature of our landed Tenures, Freeholds, Copyholds, &c. also on the Nature of our Courts of Law, and Equity, and the different Manner of proceeding in these respective Courts upon different Causes, Civil, Criminal, and Ecclesiastical. By these Means he would be able to compare the Land-holdings, and legal Processes in *England* with those Abroad, and form a truer Judgment upon his Return than most other Travellers have yet done, whether our own were better, or worse: And if worse, what might be mended, and how to do it. He would likewise then see, whether many of the Evils now complained of, are really such as could be mended without introducing greater; or whether they are of the Number of those that must be submitted to in the present imperfect State of Things. And the little Treatise lately published, called *The Analysis of the Laws of* England, seems to afford the best Assistance in this Case. If the Author shall complete the Lectures therein promised, and of which this is the Syllabus, with equal Judgment and Perspicuity (as there is great Reason to believe he will) such a Man will justly deserve the best Thanks of his Country. As to *The Present State of* England, it may be consulted occasionally in the Nature of a Dictionary, in order to see the Number of Offices, and the different Kinds of Jurisdictions exercised throughout the Kingdom.

IV. THE next Article is the legal Establishment of the Church of *England*, and a Toleration to Dissenters. A young Gentleman of a

liberal

liberal Education, especially one who is to Travel into foreign Countries, ought to know upon what Grounds a Church or Ecclesiastical Society is formed, upon what Conditions it may receive the Sanctions of the Civil Legislature, and for what Reasons, and within what Bounds, a Toleration ought to be allowed to those whose Consciences do not approve of the national Establishment. And for this Purpose Dr *Warburton*'s *Alliance between Church and State* seems to be the fittest, and to give the fullest Satisfaction of any thing yet extant. For though his System hath been greatly controverted by many, yet it hath never been properly answered or confuted. And as to making Exceptions to detached Parts of a Plan, or picking little Holes in it here and there, suffice it to say, that it is much easier to find Fault than to mend ; and that almost every Man can object, and is too naturally disposed to cavil at the Performance of another, at the same Time, that very few indeed are capable of producing an unexceptionable Plan of their own.

V. As to foreign Politics, and the Balance of Power, Dr *Campbell*'s *Present State of* Europe, has reduced all that Affair, which used to be the vague and unmeaning Talk of Coffee-house Politicians, into so regular a Science, and has fixed it upon such sure Principles, that his Treatise alone is very sufficient by way of Preparative.

VI. The last Thing is Commerce and Taxes: And as this whole Treatise pretends to enter deeply into that Matter, the less may be said in this Place. However, as it may not be amiss to take the Judgment of one or two Authors more on the same Subject, I would beg Leave to recommend Sir *J. Child* as a Commercial Writer of the first Note : And then at a respectful Distance after him, the *Remarks on the Advantages and Disadvantages of* France *and* Great Britain *in regard to Trade* may be no improper Book ; *viz.* because it exhibits a comparative View of the Commerce of both Kingdoms, and enters deeper into the Inconveniencies or Obstructions attending the *French* Government, regarding Trade, than any Author whatever. This Tract is in a great Measure a Translation of my *Essay on Trade*, and other Commercial Pieces. But as the Author is a Native of *France*, *viz.* The Marquiss *D'angeul* (though appearing under the borrowed Name of an *Englishman*, Sir *John Nicholls)* he was capable of making great Improvements on my Plan ; and being likewise imployed in the Finances, he could speak to the Difficulties and Discouragements attending Trade in that Kingdom, with more Experience and Certainty

tainty than a Stranger was capable of doing. The laſt Author re-commended is *Crouch's Book of Rates*, which is properer for a Scholar than any other (though perhaps not for the Uſe of the Merchant) becauſe it ſets forth the Improvements that have been made ſince the happy Revolution in the Syſtem of our Taxes: And becauſe it may ſuggeſt the Improvements that are ſtill to be made, by expoſing the Abſurdities which our former Princes and Parliaments committed in this Affair. Moreover when the young Traveller takes this Book with him into foreign Countries, and there compares it with their Tarifs and Syſtems of Taxation, he can determine at one Glance, whether their Taxes are better or worſe, more impoveriſhing or en-riching than ours: And conſequently, whether the Country ſo taxed, can make a Figure in Commerce, and the Arts of Peace and Induſtry, or not. For it is an indiſputable Fact, that a Progreſs in Com-merce, and that the Improvement of a Country greatly depend up-on the Nature of the national Taxes, *viz.* Whether they cramp In-duſtry, or promote it; and whether they make the Paſſion of Self-Love (that ruling Principle of human Nature) ſubſervient to the Public Good, or detrimental. In ſhort, That State or Kingdom which by means of proper Taxes converts Drones into Bees, will be Rich: But every Community which turns Bees into Drones, muſt be Poor.

WE will now ſuppoſe the young Traveller to enter upon the immediate Buſineſs of his intended Tour with theſe Accompliſh-ments: And during his Travels he ſhould conſtantly bear in mind the grand Maxim, That the Face of every Country through which he paſſes, the Looks, Numbers, and Behaviour of the People, their general Cloathing, Food, and Dwelling, their Attainments in Agri-culture, Manufactures, Arts and Sciences, are the Effects and Con-ſequences of ſome certain Cauſes; which Cauſes he was particularly ſent out to inveſtigate and diſcover. Therefore let him conſider, whether, and how far the ſaid Effects may be aſcribed to the natural Soil and Situation of the Country. — To the peculiar Genius and ſingular Inventions of the Inhabitants. — To the Public Spirit and Tenor of their Conſtitution, — or to the Religious Principles eſtabliſhed, or tolerated among them. For certain it is, that every conſiderable Effect muſt be aſcribed, and may be traced up to one or more of theſe Cauſes; which for the Sake of greater Diſtinction I will term Natural, — Artificial, — Political, — and Religious. Moreover, as it is extremely proper to aſſiſt a Beginner by raiſing ſome Queries for

him

him under each Head, it will alſo, it is humbly preſumed, not be amiſs to return ſuch Anſwers to them, as a Perſon may be ſuppoſed to give, who hath lately made the Tour both of his own, and foreign Countries, and is now ſtriking out a general Compariſon between them. For this will ſerve both to illuſtrate the Nature of the Plan, and at the ſame Time give a Sample or Specimen of the intended Manner of Proceeding. And note, Though the Scene is laid in *England*, yet the ſame Queſtions, *mutatis mutandis*, may ſerve for any Country or Climate whatever.

NATURAL CAUSES.

Q. Is the Soil of *England* naturally good and fertile, or barren and ſteril? Is it a ſhallow, or a deep Mould? inclinable to Sand, or Clay? And what ſeems to be the moſt natural Produce of the Country?

A. THE Soil is generally good, and the Mould deeper than is uſual in other Countries. Some Parts, ſuch as *Surry*, *Hampſhire*, *Norfolk*, &c. are inclinable to Sand. And others, (though of much leſs extent) are bound up with Clay. But for the moſt Part *England* hath a greater Variety of Sand, Clay, Loom, fat Earth, Marl, Chalk, Flint, Stone-Bruſh, &c. &c. within the ſame Space of Ground, perhaps the Compaſs of a County, or Hundred, nay even of a Pariſh, than moſt other Kingdoms in *Europe*; and ſeems to be a Compendium within itſelf of the Soils, Strata, Mountains, Valleys, Plains, Fens and Marſhes of other Countries. The moſt natural Produce of the Ground is Graſs, owing to the great Moiſture of the Atmoſphere. For as to the Plenty of Corn, with which *England* generally abounds, it is merely the Force of ſuperior Art and Induſtry. In regard to Minerals, the Chief are Coal, Lead, Tin, and Copper.

Q. Is the Air dry or moiſt? The Climate healthy, or ſickly? and how is it as to the Degrees of Heat, and Cold? What are the general Diſtempers of the Country? and at what particular Times of the Year do they uſually come?

A. THE Air is moiſt, the Sky ſubject to be cloudy; and the Climate remarkably mild, as to the Extremes of Heat, and Cold: But the Country cannot be pronounced ſo very healthy as ſome others Abroad. The prevalent Diſtempers are ſuch as proceed from obſtructed Perſpirations, *viz.* Scurvies, Colds, Coughs: And in Conſequence thereof, and of the Smoak of Sea Coal, Aſthmas and Conſumptions: Colds and Coughs uſually come on, when the Chills of Autumn lock up the perſpirable Matter, which uſed to paſs in the Summer.

Q. ARE

Q. ARE the married Women obſerved to be more, or leſs fruitful here than in other Countries? And do many Children die from the Birth to two Years old?

A. IT doth not appear that the married Women in *England* are altogether ſo prolific as in other Countries; and in Cities and great Towns it is certain they are remarkably otherwiſe: Whether this is to be aſcribed to the ſuperior Vice and Luxury reigning at preſent in our *Engliſh* Cities, is another Queſtion. But it is undeniable, that more Children die in *England* from the Birth to two Years old, than in any known Country whatever.

Q. How is *England* ſituated in regard to the neighbouring States and Kingdoms? Has it a free and eaſy Communication with them, by Land or Water? Or are other Countries difficult and dangerous of acceſs? What Advantages doth it derive from good Ports and Sea Carriage? and what from inland Navigation?

A. Great Britain being an Iſland is ſituated very commodiouſly between the South and North Parts of *Europe*, to hold a Communication with either: Likewiſe as it is an Iſland, the Sea, which is a conſiderable Defence againſt Invaſions, is of uſe to promote its Commerce: And the Ports are in ſuch Abundance, that there is hardly a Spot in the Kingdom above ſixty Miles diſtant from ſome Port on one Side, or other of the Iſland: As to Rivers naturally navigable, it hath not many, the *Thames*, the *Severn*, and the *Humber*, are the Chief: Some few have been rendered navigable by Art; but as the Undertakings have been carried on by private Subſcriptions, the high Tolls or Duties laid upon theſe Rivers, in order to re-imburſe the Proprietors, are a great Check to the Navigation. — If low priced Goods are to pay exceſſive Lockages, they are as effectually ſtopped from paſſing as if the Water was ſhallow, or a Bank of Sand in the Way.

Q. WHAT Improvements might be eaſily made in Matters of Water Carriage both on the Sea Coaſt, and within Land?

A. Many new Ports might be made, and others improved by building Piers, driving down Piles, *&c. &c.* at the public Expence, under the Direction of the Board of Trade. [Here ſpecify Particulars; and ſee *Lewis Morris*'s Charts for the Coaſt of *Wales*.] And the Sums ſo expended would not amount to the hundredth Part of the Money now laid out for ſecuring the uſeleſs Navigation of many Parts of *America*! The ſame Remark holds good in regard to making Rivers and Streams navigable, and cutting Canals: Not to mention, that as every Canal and navigable River are high Roads

in

in Times of Peace, fo alfo are they eafily made Fortifications in Times
of an Invafion, *viz.* By lining the Banks with a few Troops to ftop
the Progrefs of the Enemy. And the Situation of *England* is fuch,
that it might be interfected at leaft in eight or ten Places, fo as to
open a Communication with almoft every Town of Note throughout the Kingdom. The more obvious Communications are thofe,
which might be made between the Avon of *Briftol,* the *Kennet,* and
the *Thames,*—the Avon of *Briftol,* and the Avon of *Salisbury,*—the
Avon of *Briftol* and the *Thames* by way of *Letchlade* and *Cricklade,*—
alfo between the *Severn,* the *Stroud,* and [by the Help of a fhort Land
Carriage] to *Cirencefter,* and fo on to the *Thames* at *Cricklade,*—the Severn, the *Stour,* the *Penk,* the *Trent,* and the *Humber,*—the *Severn,*
the Avon [of *Stratford*] with a fmall Land Carriage to *Banbury* on
the *Charwell,* and fo to the *Ifis* at *Oxford.*—Thefe, and many fuch like
Communications might be opened in the Courfe of a few Years, by
employing fome Regiments of Soldiers during the Summer Seafons,
on each Work, and paying them fix Pence or eight Pence a Day above
their ufual Allowance.

2. WHAT other Improvements do the Situation of the Country,
the Nature of its Forefts, Heaths, Waftes, Commons, Fens and
Marfhes, readily and properly fuggeft?

A. THE Situation of the Country between the North and South,
of *Europe,* and between the Continent of *Europe* and *America,* (not
to mention *Africa* and *Afia)* plainly fhews the Feafibility of making
this Ifland become the common Depofitum, Magazine, or Storehoufe,
for each other: So that the medium Profit might be made to center.
here. As to the Royal Forefts, thefe might produce great Quantities
of Timber, were the Right of Herbage, now belonging to the adjacent Parifhes and Villages, totally abolifhed. But whilft this deftructive
Privilege remains, the Perfons interefted in the Verdure will take
effectual Care to prevent the Increafe of Timber, by fetting on Fire
the Grafs, Leaves, Fern, *&c.* in the dry Seafon, and confequently
burning the Seeds and Acorns, and deftroying all the natural Nur-
feries of young Plants. In regard to Heaths, Waftes, Commons,
Fens and Marfhes, all thefe would foon become a great Addition to
the Wealth, Strength, and Beauty of the Kingdom, were they converted into private Property, and made to yield thofe Productions,
which Nature and Providence fitted them for. Moreover, were a
great Part of the Waftes on the South Coafts from *Kent* to *Cornwall*
to be parcelled out into fmall Shares, fuppofe ten or twenty Acres, as

Portions

Portions to virtuous young Women remarkable for their Diligence in Spinning certain Quantities of Wool, Flax, or Cotton, provided they married Labourers or Farmers; this Circumstance alone would render that Country, which now looks like a desolate Wilderness, as populous and industrious as a Bee-Hive. Add to this, that were other Portions of these immense Wastes, converted into spacious Barracks well fortified, and having large Districts round them, to serve both for military Lines, and military Exercise within the Lines, in the Manner of the *Roman* Castra, with good Roads and easy Communications laid out between Barrack and Barrack; then the Consequence would be, that all the Country round would find a ready Market for their Provisions, and carry back the Soil and Manure of the Barrack or Town to raise more; — but above all, the Soldiers in these Places would be kept in good order, and properly disciplined, consequently, would be no Burden to the Innkeepers, and not be obliged, as they are at present, to take up their Quarters in Gin-Shops and Bawdy-Houses: Thus therefore, being less tainted in their Morals, Healthy, well Disciplined, and ready upon the Spot to give the Enemy a warm Reception in Case of an Invasion, to annoy him in Front, Flank, and Rear, and to defend their Fortress if besieged; they would, in all human Probability, be as great a Security to us as the Nature of this imperfect State of Things can be supposed to promise.

ARTIFICIAL CAUSES

BY the Term Artificial is here intended the Exercise and Progress of the *peculiar Genius* and inventive Powers of the Individuals in a State, considered in their *private* Capacity; whereby such Causes are distinguished from the Religious, or Political, which are more properly the united Councils of the whole Society.

AND as all Inquiries of this Sort are reduceable to two Heads, *viz.* those respecting Agriculture, and those respecting Manufactures, I shall beg Leave to suit the several Queries accordingly.

First, *Queries on the Subject of Husbandry and Agriculture.*

Q. WHAT happy Discoveries have been made of late Years in regard to Husbandry? What Improvements in turning, preparing, and dressing of Land? What new Implements, and how contrived? What Advantages and Disadvantages resulting from them?

A. THE Principles and Powers of Vegetation are still but little known; though perhaps more in *England,* and better applied to promote Husbandry and Gardening, than in most other Countries.

What

What is difcovered for certain is this, That all Vegetables, whether Herbs, Plants, Trees or Corn fuck out of the Earth, by means of their Roots and Fibres, their natural Mouths, the Particles of Food peculiar for them, and fitted for their Digeftion. They alfo imbibe the Air, Rains and Dews, by means of their Bark, Stalks and Leaves; and they carry on a Circulation, and throw off perfpirable Matter through their Pores, much in the fame Manner as Animals do. This being the Cafe, they muft have a Sufficiency of Food, or come to nothing and die. Now this Food is either got naturally on the Spot, or procured artificially from other Places. The Food got naturally, is that which is procured from the Earth, Air, Rains, Froft, and Snow, within the Reach of the Roots or Fibres, that is, the Mouths of the refpective Tree, Plant, or Herb. But even in this Cafe, the Earth, by being turned and properly ftirred, imbibes more of the Qualities of Froft and Snow, Air and Rain, than it would otherwife do : That is, it becomes more fruitful by the Help of human Induftry and Labour. Likewife this turning, digging, or plowing of the Ground at proper Seafons, befides other Ufes, deftroys the Weeds, which when thoroughly putrified, and reduced to Mould, become the Food of better and more ufeful Vegetables, fown or planted in their ftead. But for * more particular Directions, and for Cuts or Draughts of Hoes, Harrows, Plows, and other Implements, their Ufes, or Inconveniences, it would be proper to confult the principal Books on Hufbandry and Gardening, fuch as *Tull*, *Lifle*, *The complete Body of Husbandry*, *Bradley*, *Miller*, &c. And for a more analytic Theory, a chemical, and

---

* IT is next to impoffible that any Traveller could note down all that can be faid on each of thefe Heads; and it would be a mere Wafte of Time to attempt it. Neverthelefs, when a judicious Traveller meets with any thing very *fingular*, curious, or remarkable, he would do well to pay a more peculiar Attention to it, and enter down the whole Procefs of the Affair. If nothing fingular or ftriking occurs, there is no harm done; but if fomething fhould appear worth his Notice and Regard, the prefent Syftem of Queries will ferve both to fix his Attention, to improve his Reafoning, and to arrange his Thoughts and Ideas in their proper Order. And what is thus true in regard to Agriculture, Hufbandry and Vegetation, is equally true with refpect to every other Subject he will meet with in his Travels, whether Manufactures, Taxes, Politics, or Religion. Moreover, a few of the beft and choiceft Authors in every Country, and on every Subject, ought to be brought Home, in order to be confulted occafionally, and at one's Leifure: Alfo the Cuts or Draughts of Machines or Engines, where fuch are to be got, together with Defcriptions of their Ufes, and Calculations of their Expence both in making, and maintaining them.—Gentlemen, who travel after this manner, will travel to great Advantage, doing an Honour to their Country when Abroad, and to themfelves when they return Home.

and philosophical Knowledge of the Process of Nature, see Dr *Hales*'s *Vegetable Statics*, and Dr *Home*'s *Principles of Agriculture and Vegetation*.

Q. WHAT kind of Manure is applied to different Soils? How is the Manure made? from whence brought, and at what Expence?

A. MANURES of all kinds are such Food, as is prepared and brought by human Art and Industry to the Spot, where the Vegetables are growing, or designed to grow, in order to lay in a Stock for their Support and Nourishment. But as the Books of Gardening and Husbandry abovementioned are full of Rules and Directions, and will answer all Queries of this Sort, it will be properer to refer to them, than to transcribe their Words in this Place. Only let it be always remembered, that the more populous any Country is, the more Manure and Soil will be made by the Inhabitants: So that large Towns and populous Villages do not only furnish a Market for the Produce of the Country round about, and thereby pay for the Labour, and excite the Emulation of the Husbandman, but also supply him with Dung, Rags, Horn-Shavings, Ashes, Soot, &c. &c. to load his Carriages back, in order to fructify his Grounds for fresh Crops. So little Cause is there to fear, that a Country can be too populous! So empty and frivolous the Pretence of making Wars for the Sake of a greater Extent of Dominion! And such are the admirable Ways of Providence in providing for the Wants of Mankind, by the Arts of Peace and Industry, were we but to pay the Attention and Regard which are due to them!

Q. WHAT Methods are taken to water dry Grounds, or gutter wet ones? What is the Form of the Gutter, and the Expence and Manner of making it? What also are the Provisions, Machines, &c. for draining Fens and Marshes?

A. THESE Articles being Branches of Mechanics and Hydraulics, are best treated of by the Writers on the Mechanic Powers; who, together with the practical Writers on Husbandry, ought to be consulted on these Occasions. But for particular Facts, see the Account of stopping *Dagenham* Breach, draining the Fens in *Lincolnshire*, and the like.

Q. ARE the several Sorts of Grain, Seeds, Fruits, Trees, and Grasses, judiciously adapted to the Soils proper for them? Are sufficient Changes made from one Sort of Grain, Seeds, &c. to another, and from fibrous rooted Vegetables to bulbous rooted, and *vice versa*, so that the Soil may not be too fast clung together by the former, nor rendered too open and porous by the latter? Moreover, is the Grain

well

well and properly got in, and by what Inftruments, and how fecured from bad Weather, Mice, and Vermin? And how threfhed out, cleanfed and winnowed?

A. ALL thefe Inquiries are beft anfwered from Books of Hufbandry; inafmuch as it can be no Entertainment, nor much Improvement to an *Englifhman* (whatever it might be to a Foreigner) to write down thofe Particulars, which he daily fees practifed almoft in every Farm throughout the Kingdom.

2. WHAT Methods are taken for rearing Sheep, Horfes, Cattle, and for curing or preventing their Diforders; alfo for providing a Sufficiency of Food for them, efpecially at fuch Seafons of the Year, when the natural Grafs is gone?

A. SEE the Authors as before.

2. ARE Things fo contrived, as that the Raifing or Fattening of Cattle, and the Raifing of Corn fhall affift each other? And if there is any Scheme of this Nature, what is it?

A. THIS is fuch an important Article, as to deferve a peculiar Confideration. — In the South and Weft Part of *Ireland*, where Nature has been the moft liberal of her Gifts; Arts and bad Policy have brought on a general Defolation, by the fole Fact of raifing and fattening Cattle, without regard to raifing either Corn, or Flax, or Hemp, or any fuch Produce as might feed, or imploy Numbers of People: So that nothing is to be feen for many Thoufands of Acres, but Sheep and Cattle, except here and there a wretched *Irifh* Cabbin, and two or three of its miferable, half-ftarved, naked Inhabitants, to add to the Difmalnefs of the Profpect. Whereas, in *Norfolk*, a Country naturally much more barren, the People are numerous, well-cloathed, well-houfed, and well-fed; and all owing to the good Management of making the Raifing of Corn, and the Rearing, or at leaft the Fattening of Cattle, be mutually affiftant to each other. In this Country it is generally fo contrived, that the Field intended to be manured for a Crop of Corn, is not very far diftant from a Field of Turneps: And when the Sheep have fed upon the green Leaves, or when the Froft hath nipped them off, then the Field to be manured is divided into fmaller Plots by Hurdles; and twenty or thirty lean Cattle are put into a Plot: A Man is employed to draw up the Turneps, and to load a one-horfe Cart, in order to bring them to the Cattle. There he featters them about, cutting a few of them at firft into Slices, in order that they may be induced to tafte them. When they have tafted, they grow fo excefsively fond of them, as to be frequently

in

in danger of Choaking; and therefore he is provided with a Piece of Rope of a proper Size to pufh the Turnep that fticks, down their Throats. He ftrews alfo a little Hay or Straw about the Plot for the Cattle to feed on occafionally, and to prevent their Teeth from being fet on Edge by feeding altogether upon Turneps. When this Plot is fufficiently faturated with the Dung and Urine of the Animals, he moves them to another Plot, and fo on to a third, till the whole Field is fufficiently manured, and fit to be plowed up. And thus, by the Time that the Cattle are grown fat and fit for a Market, the Ground likewife is properly enriched for a Crop of Corn: And both Articles are carried on without any Inconvenience, Lofs of Time, or Expence to either; may, perhaps in a better manner, than either of them could be done feparately. As to the Turnep Field itfelf, the Feeding of the Sheep at firft upon the Greens or Tops, and the Feeding of them again upon fuch of the Turneps or Roots, as will be occafionally left, though the Majority of them are carried away, I fay, thefe two Circumftances will fufficiently enrich the Ground for fowing any common Grain, though perhaps the fafer Experiment would be to fow Barley rather than Wheat.

Q. WHAT new Markets are opened for vending the Produce of the Ground? And what Encouragements are given, or might be given, for opening more?

A. THE Bounty upon the Exportation of Corn hath opened a Market to every foreign Country, where there is any thing of Demand. But it may be made a great Query, Whether that Bounty, which in the Infancy of Agriculture was fo effentially neceffary, ought not to receive at prefent very confiderable Amendments and Reductions. And if the Legiflature fhall enact, which they feem at prefent to intend, that all Grain fhall be fold by Weight, this Circumftance will go a great Way towards redreffing the prefent Evils. As to new Markets at Home, every Road well mended produces that Effect in one Degree or other: And were more Rivers made navigable, and Canals cut, the Effects would ftill be greater and more beneficial.

Q. WHAT further Improvements in Gardening, Agriculture, and Hufbandry, might be fuggefted?

A. MANKIND in general are very flow in leaving off old Prejudices, and have a ftrong Averfion even againft thinking, much more againft publicly acknowledging, that they have ever been in the Wrong. Even at this Day there are many Parts of the Kingdom, where the Arts of Guttering of wet Lands, the proper Sowing and

Hoeing

Hoeing of Turneps, the Sowing of artificial Graſſes, raiſing of Flax and Hemp, the Uſe of the Wheel Plow, winnowing with the Toſs of the Shovel, and the ſkilful Methods of Hedging and Ditching, with many the like Improvements, have ſcarce made their Appearance.——But for a more exačt Knowledge in Gardening, Agriculture and Huſbandry, as Branches of natural Philoſophy (in order that ſuch Knowledge might hereafter deſcend to the Farmer and the Labourer) the Scheme of a Society, or Committee to be expreſſly appointed for making, receiving, and communicating Experiments, ſeems the plaineſt and the beſt.——This is a Propoſal of the Ingenious Dr *Home*, in his *Principles of Agriculture and Vegetation*, Page 173.—— And this is not the only one, by a great many, for which that worthy Gentleman deſerves the Thanks of his Countrymen, and of Mankind in general.

Secondly, *Queries on the Subječt of Trade and Manufačtures.*

Q. WHAT principal Manufačtures are carried on in this Country? and what is the Price of Labour?

A. THE principal Manufačtures are the Woollen, the Metal, (*viz.* Iron, Steel, Copper, Braſs, Tin, and Lead) the Silk, the Linnen, and the Cotton. But the Price of Labour in each Manufačture is ſo various, that it is impoſſible to give an Idea of it by any common Example. — Only it may be affirmed in general, that the Wages of Men (or what Men generally earn *per* Day) is for the moſt Part, from 1 s. to 2 s. 6 d. *per* Day; and the Wages of Women from 4 d. to 1 s. throughout the Kingdom.

Q. Do Journey-men and Journey-women work by the Day, or by the Great? And what Checks are invented to guard againſt Impoſitions of bad Work, or embezzling the Materials, or idling away Time?

A. ALMOST all Maſter Manufačturers now find it their Intereſt to pay their Work-people by the Piece, or the Great, wherever they can, rather than by the Day: Which Circumſtance alone is a ſtriking Proof, that no ſufficient Check hath yet been invented againſt the loitering away of Time, when the Maſter was to pay for it:——Not to mention, that the Perſon who works by the Day hath ſcarce any Motives to exert an Induſtry, Dexterity, or Skill ſuperior to others; whereas the Working by the Piece, or by the Great, calls them all forth; becauſe he himſelf, and none others, are to reap the Benefit and Reputation of them. [And *N. B.* this ſingle Remark, were there no others, is ſufficient to prove, that Slaves, who very literally

work

work by the Day, and can have no Motive whatever to exert any other Industry, Dexterity, or Skill, than what is just sufficient to escape the Whip of the Driver; nay, whose Self-Interest will naturally teach them to conceal any superior Talents from the Knowledge of their Masters, lest their Masters should expect a greater Task from *them* than others, and punish them for not doing it;—I say this single Remark is a full Proof, that Slaves never did, nor ever will perform their Work either so cheap, or so well, as those Freemen who work by the Piece or the Great, and are spurred on every Moment by the Examples of others, by Self-Interest, and by the Glory of excelling.] As to Checks against bad Work, the Judgment of the Master or Overseer is the best, and perhaps the only Remedy that can be applied in such a Case. But in respect to embezzling of Materials, many and various are the Methods contrived, and almost every Manufacture hath a different one; sometimes the Goods are weighed in and out, due Allowance being made for necessary Waste: At other Times Check-Engines are used to ascertain the Length or Measure, and in general Sleaing, or Weaving-Tables, are a tolerable Security against Impositions in the Weaving of Woollens, Stuffs, Linnens, Silks, Cottons, &c.

2. WHAT Machines are used to abridge the Process of a Manufacture, so that one Person can do the Work of many? And what is the Consequence of this Abridgment both regarding the Price, and the Numbers of Persons imployed?

A. FEW Countries are equal, perhaps none excel the *English* in the Numbers and Contrivance of their Machines to abridge Labour. Indeed the *Dutch* are superior to them in the Use and Application of Wind-Mills for sawing Timber, expressing Oil, making Paper, and the like. But in regard to Mines and Metals of all Sorts, the *English* are uncommonly dexterous in their Contrivance of the mechanic Powers; some being calculated for landing the Ores out of the Pits, such as Cranes and Horse-Engines:——Others for draining off superfluous Water, such as * Water Wheels and Steam Engines: Others again for easing the Expence of Carriage, such as Machines to run on inclined Planes, or Roads down Hill with wooden Frames, in order to carry many Tons of Materials at a Time. And to these must be added the various Sorts of Levers used in different Processes:

Also

---

* THE celebrated Machine of *Marli*, so much boasted of by the *French*, is but a bungling Performance in the Eyes of an *Englishman*. The same Quantity of Water might have been raised, and is raised under *London* Bridge at a fortieth Part of the Expence.

Alſo the Braſs Battery Works, the Slitting Mills, Plate, and Flatting Mills, and thoſe for making Wire of different Fineneſs. Yet all theſe, curious as they may ſeem, are little more than Preparations or Introductions for further Operations. Therefore when we ſtill conſider, that at *Birmingham*, *Woolverhampton*, *Sheffield*, and other manufacturing Places, almoſt every Maſter Manufacturer hath a new Invention of his own, and is daily improving on thoſe of others; We may aver with ſome Confidence, that thoſe Parts of *England* in which theſe Things are to be ſeen, exhibit a Specimen of practical Mechanics ſcarce to be paralleled in any Part of the World. As to Machines in the Woollen, and Stuff Way, nothing very conſiderable hath been of late attempted; owing in a great Meaſure to the miſtaken Notions of the infatuated Populace, who, not being able to ſee farther than the firſt Link of the Chain, conſider all ſuch Inventions, as taking the Bread out of their Mouths; and therefore never fail to break out into Riots, and Inſurrections, whenever ſuch Things are propoſed. In regard to the Silk Manufacture, the Throwſting Mills, eſpecially the grand one at *Derby*, are eminent Proofs of the Abridgment of that Species of Labour : And ſome Attempts have been lately made towards helping forward the Cotton and Linnen Manufactures by means of certain Engines.

In regard to the other Part of the Query, *viz.* What is the Conſequence of this Abridgment of Labour, both regarding the Price of the Goods, and the Number of Perſons imployed ? The Anſwer is very ſhort and full, *viz.* That the Price of Goods is thereby prodigiouſly lowered from what otherwiſe it muſt have been ; and that a much greater Number of Hands are imployed. The firſt of theſe is a Poſition univerſally aſſented to; but the other, though nothing more than a Corollary of the former, is looked upon by the Majority of Mankind, and even by ſome Perſons of great Name and Character, as a monſtrous Paradox. We muſt therefore endeavour to clear away theſe Prejudices Step by Step. And the firſt Step is, that Cheapneſs, *cæteris paribus*, is an Inducement to buy, — and that many Buyers cauſe a great Demand, — and that a great Demand brings on a great Conſumption; — which great Conſumption muſt neceſſarily imploy a vaſt Variety of Hands, whether the original Material is conſidered, or the Number and Repair of Machines, or the Materials out of which thoſe Machines are made, or the Perſons neceſſarily imployed in tending upon and conducting them : Not to mention thoſe Branches of the Manufacture, Package, Porterage,

Stationary

Stationary Articles, and Book-keeping, &c. &c. which muſt inevitably be performed by human Labour. But to come to ſome determinate and ſtriking Inſtance, let us take the Plow, the Harrow, the Cart, the Inſtruments for Threſhing and Winnowing, and the Mills for Grinding and Boulting, as ſo many Machines for abridging Labour in the Proceſs of making Bread; I aſk, do theſe Machines prevent, or create Imployment for the People? And would there have been as many Perſons occupied in raiſing of Corn, and making of Bread, if no ſuch Engines had been diſcovered? — The obvious Reply to this Query is, that probably the Wheaten Loaf had been confined to one, or two Families in a State, who on Account of their ſuperior Rank, and vaſt Revenues, could have afforded to give an extravagant Price for this delicious Morſel: But it is impoſſible, that under ſuch Circumſtances, it ever could have become the common Food of the Kingdom. The ſame Remark would hold good, were it to be applied to the Art of Printing, and to the Numbers of People, from firſt to laſt, therein imployed: For Printing is nothing more than a Machine to abridge the Labour, and reduce the Price of Writing.— But Examples are endleſs; and ſurely enough has been ſaid, to convince any reaſonable Man, though even the great Author of *L'Eſprit des Loix* ſhould once be of a different Mind, that that Syſtem of Machines, which ſo greatly reduces the Price of Labour, as to enable the Generality of a People to become Purchaſers of the Goods, will in the End, though not immediately, imploy more Hands in the Manufacture, than could poſſibly have found Imployment, had no ſuch Machines been invented. And every manufacturing Place, when duly conſidered, is an Evidence in this Point.

Q. Is that Labour, which is ſtill to be performed by the human Kind, ſo judiciouſly divided, that Men, Women, and Children have their reſpective Shares in Proportion to their Strength, Sex, and Abilities? And is every Branch ſo contrived, that there is no Waſte of Time, or unneceſſary Expence of Strength or Labour? Moreover, what good Conſequences attend theſe Circumſtances in ſuch Parts of the Kingdom, where they are obſerved, and what bad ones in other Parts, where they are not?

A. In many Provinces of the Kingdom, particularly, *Staffordſhire*, *Warwickſhire*, and certain Diſtricts of *Yorkſhire*, with the Towns of *Mancheſter*, *Norwich*, and ſome others, the Labour, for the moſt Part, is very properly proportioned, and great Judgment appears in the Methods and Contrivances for bringing the ſeveral Parts of the Manufacture

nufacture ſo within the Reach of each other, that no Time ſhould be waſted in paſſing the Goods to be manufactured from Hand to Hand, and that no unneceſſary Strength ſhould be imployed. For an Inſtance of both Kinds, take one among a Thouſand at *Birmingham*, *viz.* When a Man ſtamps a metal Button by means of an Engine, a Child ſtands by him to place the Button in readineſs to receive the Stamp, and to remove it when received, and then to place another. By theſe means the Operator can ſtamp at leaſt double the Number, which he could otherwiſe have done, had he been obliged to have ſtopped each Time to have ſhifted the Buttons: And as his Gettings may be from 14 *d.* to 18 *d.* and the Child's from a Penny to 2 *d. per* Day for doing the ſame Quantity of Work, which muſt have required double the Sum, had the Man alone been imployed; this ſingle Circumſtance ſaves above 80, or near 100 *per Cent.* at the ſame Time that it trains up Children to an Habit of Induſtry, almoſt as ſoon as they can ſpeak. And hence it is, that the *Bijoux d'Angleterre*, or the *Birmingham* Toys, are rendered ſo exceedingly cheap as to aſtoniſh all *Europe*; and that the Roman Catholic Countries are ſupplied with ſuch vaſt Quantities of Crucifixes, Agnus Dei's, *&c.* from *England*. A Dozen of theſe Crucifixes, as I am informed, being to be ſold, in the wholeſale Way, for 7½ *d.* — But the good Effects of this proportioning of Labour to different Strengths and Sexes, is ſtill more extenſive than it firſt appears. For in *Birmingham* the Numbers of poor Women on the Pay-Bill, compared to thoſe of poor Men, are hardly as three to two; whereas in *Briſtol*, where no ſuch good Polities obtain, the Numbers are upwards of four to one; and in many Parts of *London*, it is ſtill much worſe: So great is the Difference, and ſuch the Expenſiveneſs and heavy Burdens of a wrong Conduct even in this Reſpect: not to mention, that Proſtitution and Debauchery ſeem to be an unavoidable Conſequence in the female Sex of Poverty and Idleneſs, when they are young; and when they grow old, what Refuge can they have, if they do not ſoon rot with their Diſeaſes, but the Pariſh Pay?

2. In thoſe Towns and Places, where great Manufactures are carried on, are there many independent Maſters, and few Journeymen to each Maſter? or few independent Maſters, and many Journeymen? And what is the Difference, in regard to Morals, Cheapneſs and Goodneſs of Work, Extent of Trade, Rioting, Mobbing and the like?

A. This

A. THIS Matter is better illuſtrated by comparing the ſame Manufacture, and the Conſequences attending it, under the different Circumſtances here referred to. In many Parts of *Yorkſhire*, the Woollen Manufacture is carried on by ſmall Farmers and Freeholders: Theſe People buy ſome Wool, and grow ſome; their Wives, Daughters, and Servants ſpin it in the long Winter Nights, and at ſuch Times when not imployed in their Farms and Dairies; the Maſter of the Family either ſells this Produce in the Yarn Market, or hath it wove up himſelf. It is then milled, cleanſed, and brought to Market, generally to the Town of *Leeds*; but when ſold there, he can be paid for no greater Number of Yards than the Cloth will meaſure after having been well ſoaked in Water: By which means all Frauds in Stretching, Tentering, &c. are effectually prevented. The Perſons who buy this Cloth, generally act upon Commiſſion at a very low Rate; and afterwards cauſe the Cloth to be dyed (if it was not dyed in the Wool) and to be properly dreſſed and finiſhed. Thus, the whole paſſes through various Hands independently of each other. And though in Fact the Spinner, Weaver, Millman, Dyer, Dreſſer, &c. &c. are all of them the Journeymen of the Agent or Commiſſioner, who ſtands in the Stead of him who is the Clothier in other Places; yet by acting thus upon a diſtinct Footing, they conceive themſelves as far independent of him, and of each other, as any Buyer or Seller whatever: And being thus independent, they are all Rivals, all animated with the ſame Deſire of bringing their Goods to Market upon the cheapeſt Terms, and of excelling one another. Their Journeymen likewiſe, if they have any, being ſo little removed from the Degree and Condition of their Maſters, and ſo likely to ſet up for themſelves by the Induſtry and Frugality of a few Years, have no Conception that they are embarked in an Intereſt oppoſite to that of their Maſters, or that they are called upon to enter into Clubs and Combinations againſt them. Thus it is, that the working People are generally Moral, Sober, and Induſtrious; that the Goods are well made, and exceedingly Cheap; and that a Riot or a Mob is a Thing hardly known among them. Whereas in *Gloceſterſhire*, *Wiltſhire*, and *Somerſetſhire*, the Manufacture is carried on by a quite different Proceſs, and the Effects are accordingly; *viz.* One Perſon, with a great Stock and large Credit, buys the Wool, pays for the Spinning, Weaving, Milling, Dying, Shearing, Dreſſing, &c. &c. That is, he is the Maſter of the whole Manufacture from firſt to laſt, and perhaps imploys a thouſand Perſons under him. This is the Clothier,

whom

whom all the Rest are to look upon as their Paymaster. But will they not also sometimes look upon him as their Tyrant? And as great Numbers of them work together in the same Shop, will they not have it the more in their Power to vitiate and corrupt each other, to cabal and associate against their Masters, and to break out into Mobs and Riots upon every little Occasion? The Event hath fully shewed, and is now shewing, that these Conjectures are too frequently supported by Facts. Besides, as the Master is placed so high above the Condition of the Journeyman, both their Conditions approach much nearer to that of a Planter and Slave in our *American* Colonies, than might be expected in such a Country as *England*; and the Vices and Tempers belonging to each Condition are of the same Kind, only in an inferior Degree. The Master, for Example, however well-disposed in himself, is naturally tempted by his Situation to be proud and over-bearing, to consider his People as the Scum of the Earth, whom he has a Right to squeeze whenever he can; because they ought to be kept low, and not to rise up in Competition with their Superiors. The Journeymen on the contrary, are equally tempted by their Situation, to envy the high Station, and superior Fortunes of their Masters; and to envy them the more, in Proportion as they find themselves deprived of the Hopes of advancing themselves to the same Degree by any Stretch of Industry, or superior Skill. Hence their Self-Love takes a wrong Turn, destructive to themselves, and others. They think it no Crime to get as much Wages, and to do as little for it as they possibly can, to lie and cheat, and do any other bad Thing; provided it is only against their Master, whom they look upon as their common Enemy, with whom no Faith is to be kept. The Motives to Industry, Frugality, and Sobriety are all subverted by this one Consideration, *viz.* That they shall always be chained to the same Oar, and never be but Journeymen. Therefore their only Happiness is to get Drunk, and to make Life pass away with as little Thought as possible. This being the Case, is it to be wondered at, that the Trade in *Yorkshire* should flourish, or the Trade in *Somersetshire*, *Wiltshire*, and *Glocestershire* be found declining every Day? The real Surprize would be to discover, that such Causes did not produce such Effects: And if ever the Manufacturers in the North should adopt the bad Policy of the West, and *vice versa*, Things will come round again.

2. ARE the Manufactures of *England*, those especially in the Toy, Jewelry, Cabinet, Furniture, and Silk Way, chiefly adapted for high

or

or middling Life? and what Species of People make up the Bulk of the Customers?

A. England being a free Country, where Riches got by Trade are no Disgrace, and where Property is also safe against the Prerogative either of Prince or Nobles, and where every Person may make what Display he pleases of his Wealth, without incurring a higher *Taille*, Poll, or Capitation the next Year for so doing;—the Manufactures of the Kingdom accommodate themselves, if I may so speak, to the Constitution of it: That is, they are more adapted for the Demands of Peasants and Mechanics, in order to appear in warm Circumstances;—for Farmers, Freeholders, Tradesmen, and Manufacturers in middling Life;—and for wholesale Dealers, Merchants, and all Persons of Landed Estates, to appear in genteel Life; than for the Magnificence of Palaces, or the Cabinets of Princes. Thus it is, according to the very Spirit of our Constitution, that the *English* of these several Denominations have better Conveniencies in their Houses, and affect to have more in Quantity of clean, neat Furniture, and a greater Variety (such as Carpets, Screens, Window Curtains, Chamber Bells, polished Brass Locks, Fenders, &c. &c. Things hardly known Abroad among Persons of such a Rank) than are to be found in any other Country in *Europe, Holland* excepted. Moreover, as the Demand is great and continual, the Numbers of Workmen and their greater Experience excite the higher Emulation, and cause them to excel the Mechanics of other Countries in these Sorts of Manufactures. In a Word, it is a true Observation, that almost the whole Body of the People of *Great Britain* may be considered either as the Customers *to*, or the Manufacturers *for* each other: A very happy Circumstance this, on which the Wealth and Prosperity of a Nation greatly depends.——Were an Inventory to be taken of the Houshold Goods and Furniture of a Peasant, or Mechanic in *France*, and of a Peasant, or Mechanic in *England*, the latter would be found, upon an Average, to exceed the former in Value at least as three to one.

Q. In what particular Manufactures, Arts, or Sciences, are the *English* Nation chiefly deficient?

A. They are said to be out-done by Foreigners in most of the higher or politer Arts, such as Painting, Engraving, Statuary, and Music. And one Reason seems to be, that neither the Religion, nor Political Constitution of the Country give that Encouragement to these Studies, which is to be met with Abroad; our Churches, for Example, admitting of little more than elegant Neatness; and our

Situation, as an Island, besides other Circumstances, preventing our Artists from taking Models, or trying their Ingenuity in the Palaces of foreign Princes.

_Q._ ARE there any peculiar Institutions, or voluntary Societies erected with a View to give Incouragement, and distribute Premiums to those who shall excel in the mechanic Arts, and Manufactures?

A. Ireland seems to have been the first Place in the _British_ Empire, which had the Honour of giving Birth to Institutions of this Nature. But now there is a numerous Society of Noblemen, and Gentlemen, formed in _London_ for promoting Arts, Manufactures, and Commerce. The _Antigallican_ Societies are likewise much upon the same Plan; except that they take in likewise the discouraging the Consumption of _French_ Wine, and Use of their Manufactures. The Society of _Edinburgh_ comprehends not only Arts and Manufactures, but also Agriculture, and the Study of Vegetation. And that at _Glasgow_, as I am informed, is intended to promote the finer Arts in Conjunction with the others. Moreover, the Gentlemen of _Brecknockshire_ in the Principality of _Wales_, came to a very laudable Resolution, about two Years ago, of converting a monthly Hunting Club into " A Society for encouraging Improvements in Agriculture " and Manufactures, and promoting the general Good of the " Country." And the Success, which hath already attended this Institution, affords great Hopes, that many other Clubs and Societies throughout the Kingdom, will follow their Example, and convert themselves into public-spirited Institutions of real Use, and extensive Benefit.

POLITICAL CAUSES.

THESE being as extensive as they are important, ought to be subdivided into separate Heads; _viz._ Such as constitute the Rights, Privileges, and Liberties of the Subject; — such as establish the national Taxes; — and such others, which being compounded of all Parts of the Constitution operating together, may be termed the Spirit or Essence of it.

Queries relating to the Rights, Liberties and Privileges of the Subject.

_Q._ WHAT are those Rights and Privileges of an _Englishman_, which seem peculiar to him, and whereby he may be distinguished from the Subject of another State?

A. Englishmer,

A. Engliſhmen, as ſuch, have ſeveral Privileges of a very valuable and extenſive Nature ; as *Firſt*, Every Man hath the ſame equal Security, one as well as another, againſt arbitrary Impriſonments : That is, no Perſon, though the higheſt in the Kingdom, can impriſon or detain the meaneſt, without alledging ſome legal Cauſe, and bringing that Cauſe to a judicial Hearing : And the ſame Obſervation may be applied to Security of Poſſeſſions againſt any Invader, as well as Security of Perſon. *Secondly*, When a Subjeƈt is accuſed of any Crime, of what Nature ſoever, the Accuſers or Witneſſes muſt appear Face to Face in open Court, to be interrogated by him concerning the ſame ; and he himſelf, after he hath finiſhed his Defence, is then to be judged by Twelve of his Peers (*i. e.* by Perſons of the ſame Condition, or nearly the ſame with himſelf) whether guilty, or not. *Thirdly*, He can have no Taxes levied upon him, but ſuch as he is ſuppoſed to agree or conſent to by his Proxy or Repreſentative in the Houſe of Commons, *i. e.* by the Member, or Members, of Parliament for the County, City, or Borough to which he belongs.

Q. WHAT are the Forms or Proceſſes of Law, or general Methods of proceeding in Civil, Criminal, or Eccleſiaſtical Cauſes ? And what Inſtitutions might be borrowed from other Countries to render our Law Proceedings more certain, and expeditious, more adequate to natural Juſtice, and attended with leſs Chicane, and leſs Expence ?

A. As to the former Part of the Query, a great deal depends at preſent upon that Knowledge which is to be gained by perſonal Experience, and Attendance in the Courts ; there being no Treatiſe yet extant, as far as I can learn, to explain theſe Matters in a full and diſtinƈt Manner. But for a general or compendious Knowledge of them, ſee *The Analyſis of the Laws of* England, Books III. and IV. *viz.* " Of private Wrongs and civil Injuries ; and of public Wrongs and " Miſdemeanors." In regard to the latter Part of the Query, the Author freely confeſſes, that he is not able to anſwer it : His Stay abroad having been too ſhort, and too much taken up with other Avocations, to have acquired a ſufficient Inſight into theſe Matters : But the Query nevertheleſs may have its Uſe in a Treatiſe of this Nature, as it is to ſtand to be anſwered by thoſe, who ſhall have more Time and Leiſure, ſhall viſit more Countries, and can turn their Thoughts particularly to this Subjeƈt.

Q. Are Tradeſmen and Plebeians in *England* equally at Liberty to purchaſe landed Eſtates with Gentlemen or Noblemen ? And are

there

there any territorial Jurisdiction annexed to them? What likewise is the Power of Landlords over their Tenants?

A. ALL natural born Subjects of the Realm are upon an equal Footing as to the Liberty of purchasing, if they have the Ability. But as to territorial or hereditary Jurisdictions, there is scarce such a Thing now remaining in any Part of the Kingdom; those in *Scotland* being lately purchased, and annexed to the Crown. Indeed, the Courts Leet and Courts Baron, together with the Payments of Herriots and Services still required in some Places, may be said to keep up the Shadow of the antient *Gothic* Constitution of Baron and Vassal; but the Substance of that Tyranny and Slavery is pretty well destroyed; and these customary Duties, Services, &c. are expiring every Day: So that in short, the Tenant who pays his Rent, has as little to fear from his Landlord, as from any other Person.

Q. WHAT Incouragements, Exemptions, Privileges, or Honours are granted to the married State? And what Discouragements, Burdens, or Dishonours laid on the contrary?

A. None, or next to none either Way, to the very great Detriment and dispeopling of the Country, Corruption of Morals, and Reproach of the Legislature. This Omission is the more to be lamented, as the very Nature of our Government, and Form of our Constitution, point out such easy and effectual Remedies; *viz.* to annex the Privileges of Voting, and the Posts of Honour and Profit to the married State; and to compel Batchelors of a certain Age, suppose Thirty, to pay double Taxes in all Respects whatever, *viz.* Land, Window, Coach, Plate, Church and Poor, Tithes, and all County Taxes, Excise, and Customs, and to be obliged to serve all Offices of Burden and Expence.

Q. AS Lands are best cultivated, when divided into moderate Shares, and that Country is the richest and most populous, and consequently the strongest, which hath the greatest Number of Freeholders and middling Gentry residing in it; What Polities are established by the Constitution to prevent the monopolizing of landed Property into a few Hands? What Care is also taken to make reasonable and judicious Wills for those who die Intestate? or in other Words, to divide the Estates of such Persons agreeably to the Laws of right Reason and Equity among their Children, or nearest of Kin?

A. The Constitution hath established no Polity whatever to prevent Monopolies of this Sort; but on the contrary, hath encouraged

and

and increaſed the natural Vanity of Mankind towards raiſing one Perſon to be the Head of the Family to the Impoveriſhing, and ſometimes Beggaring of all the reſt.——To trace this Affair to its true Source, we ſhall find that in *England*, before the *Norman* Conqueſt, ſuch landed Eſtates, *as had no civil or martial Juriſdiction belonging to them*, were made to deſcend equally among all the Children, like as Goods and Chattels do now. This was, it muſt be owned, running too far into the *Agrarian* Scheme of Levelling and Equality; and had certainly ſome Inconvenience attending it: For it cannot be at all proper, that ſuch a Syſtem ſhould take Place, in any Monarchy of conſiderable Extent. But on the other Hand, when the *Normans* took Poſſeſſion of the *Engliſh* Eſtates, they introduced their own Cuſtoms, which gave *all* to the Eldeſt, and none to the reſt of the Children: So that the Conſtitution was totally changed from one Extreme to the other. But though ſomething might be urged at that Juncture in behalf of the *Normans*, who by erecting almoſt all Eſtates into Knight's Fees, could the eaſier keep the *Engliſh* in Subjection; inaſmuch as every Knight was bound, when ſummoned, to appear with his military Tenants, to defend the Poſſeſſions of his immediate Lord; — I ſay though this might be a good Plea for the *Normans* under ſuch Circumſtances, What Plea can it be for us at this Diſtance of Time, and in ſo different a Situation? Or is it really intended, by the late Clamours for a national Militia, to recur to the old Methods of making the ſame Perſon the hereditary Colonel of his Tenants, as well as their Landlord? If this is the Caſe, it may be a good Reaſon upon ſuch Grounds, why the eldeſt Son ought to have all the Eſtate, and the reſt none:—— But at the ſame time it affords a very ſtrong Argument againſt ſo great an Incroachment on our preſent Rights and Liberties, as ſuch a national Militia muſt certainly be. In ſhort, the preſent *Engliſh* Practice of giving all to the Eldeſt, appears the more abſurd, if we farther conſider, that even in *France* itſelf, where Notions of high Birth and the Pride of Family certainly run ſufficiently high, the Cuſtoms of *Normandy* are not the Cuſtoms of the reſt of the Kingdom. For in ſome Provinces, the eldeſt Son hath two thirds; in others he hath only one half, and then comes in for a Child's Share in the Diviſion of the Remainder. And this Practice, which I think obtains in all *Guienne*, a Country full of Nobleſſe, is attended with no Inconvenience whatſoever. Why therefore ſhould it not be introduced into *England*, a Country more particularly ſubſiſting by Commerce and Navigation? And why, in

the

the Name of Common Senfe, fhould the *Norman* Cuftom, fo repugnant to the Reft of our Conftitution, be continued any longer among us. [See *The Elements of Commerce*, Pages 44, 47.]—To illuftrate this Reafoning yet farther, we may obferve, That the Cuftom of *Paris* is pure Gavelkind, or equal Divifion; a Cuftom not improper for Commercial Cities, or little Republics; and indeed highly requifite in fmall Iflands, in order to prevent over-grown Landed Eftates, and to keep all the Inhabitants in a State of Induftry; a Cuftom alfo the moft effectual of any towards peopling new Colonies:—Now this is the very Cuftom which the *French* Government hath judicioufly introduced into all their Sugar Colonies; by Virtue of which, thefe Iflands are well-peopled, well-defended, well-cultivated, and very affiftant to their Mother Country: Their Sugars alfo, Indigo, and Coffee, are better in Quality, and infinitely more in Quantity, and are almoft *Cent. per Cent.* cheaper, Sugars efpecially, than any that come from our Plantations: Though, *N. B.* they buy their Negroes, their Lumber, and Provifions at a much dearer Rate than our Planters do. *Jamaica*, on the contrary, is as thinly peopled as ever; and the Inhabitants, inftead of affording any military Affiftance to the Mother Country, are under perpetual Alarms of being deftroyed by their own Negroes. Add to this, that the Expences which *Great Britain* hath been at in Fleets and Forces to protect *Jamaica*, and the Reft of the Sugar Iflands, from foreign Invafions for thefe twenty Years laft paft, are almoft incredible. Moreover, as to the Reft of the *Englifh* Sugar Iflands, Land is monopolizing, and the white Inhabitants are growing thinner every Day. This is the Fact; and a Fact too quite the Reverfe of the *French*. Judge therefore from thefe Circumftances, as we have paid fo dearly for our Knowledge, and are ftill paying, whether we ought not to grow wifer, than to fuffer the *Norman* Cuftoms to prevail any longer in our Sugar Iflands. — For furely, *Fas eft & ab hofte doceri.*

Q. WHAT good Laws regarding Commerce and Manufactures are now in Force? And what Bounties and Premiums are given to fupport Manufactures in their Infant State?

A. As to the firft Part of this Query, it muft be obferved, that there are very few, if any Laws fubfifting for that Purpofe: Nor indeed is there that Neceffity for them (I mean Laws of the *pofitive* Kind) which the Generality of Men are apt to imagine. For let the Legiflature but take Care not to make *bad Laws*, and then as to *good ones*, they will make themfelves: That is, the Self-Love and Self-Intereft

of

of each Individual will prompt him to feek fuch Ways of Gain, Trades, and Occupations of Life, as by ferving himfelf, will promote the public Welfare at the fame Time. The only Thing neceffary to be done by pofitive Inftitutions is, to enforce the Obfervance of voluntary Contracts by legal Penalties fpeedily levied. Thus, for Example, If a Man contracts a Debt, he ought to be obliged to pay it in a Manner the leaft burdenfome to the Creditor: And Debts contracted for Goods or Merchandife ought to have the Preference of all others. Moreover, if he fells Goods by Samples, the Goods fold ought not to be worfe than the Samples; and the fame Remark will extend to the Selling of Goods by the Piece, or in the wholefale Way: Becaufe the outward Appearance of fuch Goods ought to be confidered as a Sample of the inward Reality of them. And therefore, if they fhould prove to be worfe than they *appeared*, having Flaws or Blemifhes concealed within, or if they fhould be fhort of Meafure, Weight, &c. the Seller ought to make ample Reparation to the Buyer, and be fubject likewife to fome Fine, or Mark of Infamy. But in Fact, fuch Laws as thefe are Laws of *Juftice*, rather than of Commerce; and therefore cannot be faid to promote its Intereft, or the Intereft of Manufactures, in any other Way, than as all Things neceffarily do, which oblige us to do to others, as we would be done by. Indeed, it muft be acknowledged with Gratitude and Pleafure, that the Legiflature of late Years hath enacted many excellent Laws which have promoted Commerce, increafed Induftry, and extended Manufactures. This, I fay, ought ever to be acknowledged; but then the Laws in Queftion are fuch, whofe true Excellence confifts rather in the Repeal of abfurd and bad Laws formerly made, than in any particular Pofitions or Maxims of Commerce: And as to the pernicious Statutes formerly enacted, many fuch, as will foon appear, there are ftill remaining, which ought to be repealed.

In regard to the other Part of the Query, *viz.* " What Bounties " or Premiums are given to fupport Trades and Manufactures in " their Infant State?" The Anfwer is, That the Inftitutions of Bounties, Premiums, and Drawbacks, are in a Manner peculiar to *Great Britain* and *Ireland*; there being more of them introduced into our Commercial Syftem within thefe fixty Years, than are to be met with in all *Europe* befides. And thefe Incouragements are of two Sorts, *viz.* Firft, fuch as are granted upon Manufactures, or fuperabundant Produce to promote the *Exportation* of them; and fecondly, fuch as are given upon Raw Materials growing in our own Colonies, to

promote

promote the *Importation* of them. In regard to the former, we ought to diſtinguiſh between Bounties, and Drawbacks; the one being a Sum actually given or paid by the People in general to particular Exporters; the other being no more than a Return of that Tax or Duty upon Exportation, which was, or would have been levied upon the Goods, if uſed for home Conſumption. Now the Commodities entitled to Bounties are at preſent Corn, and Spirits diſtilled from Corn, Fiſh, and Fleſh, Gunpowder, coarſe Linnens, Sail-Cloth, and ſome Sorts of Silk Manufactures: To which may be added, as peculiar Caſes, the Bounty on the Tonnage of Ships employed in the Royal *Britiſh*, and the *Greenland* Fiſheries. — The Commodities entitled to Drawbacks are, refined Sugars, Sope, Candles, Starch, Leather, and Leather Manufactures, Paper, Ale, Mum, Cyder, Perry, alſo Spirituous Liquors, wrought Plate, Gold and Silver Lace, and Glaſs. Alſo [foreign] Silks, Callicoes, Linnens, and Stuffs, if printed, painted, ſtained, or dyed in *Great Britain*. The Commodities or raw Materials coming from our Colonies entitled to a Bounty, are Pitch, Tar, and Turpentine, Naval Stores, and Indigo. — Now upon a Review of theſe ſeveral Articles, it is eaſy to ſee, that all our Manufactures ought to be exported *Duty free*; and therefore, the Inſtitution of Drawbacks, or Return of Duties, ſhould always make a Part in the Commercial Syſtem of every wiſe Government: It is alſo eaſy to ſee, that ſuch infant Manufactures, or raw Materials, as promiſe to become hereafter of general Uſe and Importance, ought to be reared and nurſed during the Weakneſs and Difficulties of their infant State, by public Incouragements and national Premiums. But it doth by no means ſo clearly appear, that this nurſing and ſupporting ſhould be *continued for ever*. On the contrary, it ſeems more natural to conclude, that after a reaſonable Courſe of Years, Attempts ought to be made to wean this commercial Child by gentle Degrees, and not to ſuffer it to contract a lazy Habit of leaning continually on the leading Strings. In ſhort, all Bounties to particular Perſons are juſt ſo many Taxes upon the Community; and that particular Trade is not worth the having, which never can be brought to ſupport itſelf. Were all Manufactures to receive a Bounty (and all have equal right to expect it) this Reaſoning would appear unanſwerable.

2. WHAT bad Laws relating to Trade and Manufactures are now ſubſiſting?

A. A PRODIGIOUS Number, as will appear by the following Detail.

1. ALL

1. ALL Laws and exclusive Privileges whatever; all Constitutions of Companies of Trade, Corporations, &c. &c. relating to the internal Commerce of the Kingdom: under which Head must likewise be comprehended that absurd Statute of the fifth of Queen *Elizabeth*, which restrains Persons from exercising those very Trades they may have the happiest Genius for, and in which they may have made great Improvements, and excelled all that went before them.—Yet, strong and unanswerable as these Reasons are, they are totally over-ruled by this single Law; and the unfortunate, ingenious Person, must be debarred from exercising that Trade, which Nature herself designed him for, and perhaps in which only he could be of use to his Country; because, forsooth, he had not served a regular Apprenticeship! But the pernicious Tendency of these several Restraints have been made more amply to appear in *The Elements of Commerce*, Pages 79—92.

2. ALL Statutes and exclusive Charters made for the Shackling and Confinement of foreign Trade, must undoubtedly come under the Denomination of bad, nay, the worst of Laws. In relation to which see *The Elements of Commerce*, Pages 93—135.

3. THE Statutes relating to Pauper Settlements, are another great Confinement and Disadvantage to Trade; without being of real Benefit to any Set of Men whatever, the Lawyers excepted. See *The Elements of Commerce*, Pages 20—21.

4. THE Statutes for the due ordering and making particular Sorts of Goods, keeping them up to a Standard, regulating their Lengths and Breadths, appointing of what Materials, or at what Seasons of the Year they shall be made, &c. &c. are also a useless Farce and Burden; and only serve now and then as an Handle for one litigious, or lazy Rival, to vex his industrious, or ingenious Neighbour. For as to general Use, they are absolutely impracticable; and ever will so remain, as long as Buyers and Sellers vary in their Prices, Fancies, Tastes, &c. In one Word, if the Buyer is not *deceived* in buying them (that is, if they shall prove throughout such as they *appear* to be, and are in reality the same he bought them for) it is of no sort of Consequence when, or how, or where, or with what Materials they were made, or whether the Goods are longer or shorter, broader or narrower, coarser or finer, better or worse, than those usually made before them. See *The Elements of Commerce*, Page 88.

5. LASTLY, The Statutes for regulating Wages and the Price of Labour, are another Absurdity, and a very great Hurt to Trade. — Absurd and preposterous it must surely appear, for a third Person

to

to attempt to fix the Price between Buyer and Seller, without their own Confents: For if either the Journeyman will not fell his Labour at the fixed or ſtatutable Price, or the Maſter will not give it, of what Uſe are a thouſand regulating Laws? Nay, how indeed can any ſtated Regulations be ſo contrived, as to make due and reaſonable Allowance for Plenty or Scarcity of Work, Cheapneſs or Dearneſs of Proviſions, Difference of living in Town or Country, Firing, Houſe-Rent, &c &c. alſo for the Goodneſs or Badneſs of the Workmanſhip, the different Degrees of Skill or Diſpatch of the Workman, the unequal Goodneſs of Materials to work upon, State of the Manufacture, and the Demand, or Stagnation at Home or Abroad? I ſay, How is it poſſible to make due Allowance for all theſe various and contingent Circumſtances? And yet, were even this poſſible, a great Difficulty ſtill recurs, *viz.* Who ſhall, or how can you force the Journeyman to work, or the Maſter to give him Work, unleſs they themſelves ſhall mutually agree about it? — And if they agree, why ſhould you, or I, or any one elſe interfere? and what need of any Regulations at all? In ſhort, ſuch Laws as theſe can do no good, becauſe they never can be carried into a regular, uſeful Practice: But on the contrary, they may cauſe a great deal of Miſchief, Riots, and Diſturbances; and will infallibly, ſooner or later, drive the Trade from that Country, where Men are abſurd enough to attempt to put them in Execution.

Now this being the Caſe, and theſe the Numbers of bad and pernicious Laws, it is very evident, that were they all repealed, one farther good Conſequence would reſult, beſides thoſe already mentioned, *viz.* our *Statutes at Large,* as they are juſtly called, would not appear of ſo enormous a Bulk as they now do. For perhaps a fourth, if not a third Part of their Number would be found upon Examination to be no other than Statutes relating either to Companies of Trades, and the Freedoms of Corporations at Home, — or to excluſive Companies for trading Abroad, — or to Pauper and Pariſh Settlements — or to the keeping of Manufactures to ſome ſuppoſed particular Standard, — or to regulate Wages and the Price of Labour. Therefore the ſooner all theſe were repealed and aboliſhed, the better for the Public in every Reſpect. — As they ſtand at preſent, they are the Reproach and Nuſance of a Free People, and the Plague of a Commercial Nation.

Queries

Queries relating to the Nature and Tendency of the National Taxes.

Q. As Taxes muſt be levied in all Countries for the Defence and Support of the State, — What conſtitutes a good Tax, and what a bad one ?

A. A good Tax is that which tends to prevent Idleneſs, check Extravagance, and promote Induſtry : A bad Tax, on the contrary, falls the heavieſt of all upon the induſtrious Man, excuſing, or at leaſt not puniſhing the Idle, the Spend-thrift, or the Vain.   Taxes therefore when properly laid on, muſt enrich a Country ; but when improperly, will as certainly impoveriſh it ; and the Sum produced into the Exchequer ought not to be ſo much the principal Conſideration, as the Nature and Tendency of the Tax. — Only it may be obſerved as a Corollary of what hath been here ſaid, that an improper Tax can never amount to any conſiderable Sum ; becauſe it impoveriſhes the Country, and by that Means diſables the People from paying it.   Whereas a proper Tax, by cauſing Induſtry to flouriſh, by preventing Idleneſs, and checking Extravagance, is itſelf the Cauſe of that Riches which flow ſo abundantly into the Exchequer. — A Manufacturer, for Inſtance, if prevented by a judicious Tax from getting frequently drunk even with the cheapeſt Ale, or Gin, till he arrives at thirty five, or forty Years of Age ; and if he is careful and induſtrious in the mean while, — may afterwards very probably be able to afford a Bottle of good Wine every Day at his Table, with Houſe, and Furniture, and all Things ſuitable thereto : And yet neither do himſelf, nor his Family any real Diſſervice. Such is the Difference both to a Man's Self, and to the Public, between ſpending properly, and improperly : And ſo true it is, that Sobriety and Induſtry, at the long run, will contribute infinitely more in Taxes to the Support of the State, than Idleneſs, Drunkenneſs, or Extravagance.

Q. ARE all Perſons, from the higheſt to the loweſt, impartially taxed ? Or are ſome Individuals, ſome Ranks and Orders of Men, or certain Towns and Diſtricts, exempted from paying one, or more of the National Taxes ?

A. England is much happier than moſt other Countries in regard to the univerſal Diſtribution and Impartiality of the Taxes ; there being hardly any Exemptions or Privileges to one Perſon, to one Claſs, or Degree of Men, to one Town or Diſtrict, more than another. — Indeed, the Nobility and higher Gentry have ſome little,

ſmall Indulgence ſhewn them in the Affair of the Coach and Plate
Tax: But theſe are Things ſo very inconſiderable, if compared with
the large Exemptions that take Place in every Country abroad (*Holland* perhaps excepted) that they are not worth naming. Be it rather obſerved, as a thing of much greater Conſequence, that ſuch
partial Exemptions, in Proportion as they obtain, are ever found to
impoveriſh a Country, and to cauſe all the uſeful, manufacturing,
and mercantile People to grow weary of their Trades, and to run mad
after Nobility. And of the Truth of this *France* itſelf affords too
many Inſtances; *Germany* ſtill more; *Hungary* more than *Germany*:
and *Poland* the moſt of all. And what is the Conſequence? — Why
truly, *Hungary* and *Poland*, naturally two of the beſt, fineſt, and
moſt fruitful Countries in *Europe*, are rendered by this wretched Art
and bad Policy the pooreſt and moſt miſerable of all.

Q. ARE any Taxes laid upon the Paſſage or Tranſport of Mer-
chandiſe from one Place, one County, or Province of the Kingdom to
another? Or may they paſs free of any Tolls, Town Duties, or other
Burdens; — thoſe only excepted which are appropriated to repair the
Roads, and facilitate the Carriage?

A. HERE again *England* hath a great Advantage over moſt other
Countries; inaſmuch as all the old, narrow Methods of Tolls, and
Town Duties, and other Contrivances for ſtopping the Circulation
of mutual Induſtry and Labour, are deſervedly exploded; ſo that
hardly any Footſteps remain of this antient, *Gothic*, barbarous Cuſ-
tom. Whereas in every Kingdom abroad, not excepting *France* itſelf, the Tolls, Town Duties, Cuſtoms, and other Impoſitions, have
a moſt baleful Influence in ſtopping the Carriage of a Manufacture
from one neighbouring Town, or Province, to the other. — And if
Manufactures are prevented from being carried in order to be ex-
changed with each other, or in other Words, to be bought and ſold,
they are prevented from being made; and ſo much Labour is loſt to
the Community.

Q. UNDER what Heads might the National Taxes be the moſt
properly ranged?

A. To omit leſſer Diviſions, they may be ranged with ſufficient
Accuracy for the preſent Purpoſe, under the Land Tax — the ſeveral
Branches collected by the Officers of Exciſe (under which the Salt
may be likewiſe comprehended) — and the Stamp Duties.

Q. WHICH

Q. WHICH of thefe feveral Duties do come under the Definition of good Taxes as above laid down; and ought therefore to be continued; — Which alfo are bad Taxes, and ought to be repealed?

A. THE Land Tax is become of late Years, a moft excellent Tax for the exciting of Induftry, and all kinds of Improvements; inafmuch as the Increafe of Produce and Advancements of Value pay no higher a Tax, than the Grounds would have paid, had there been no Improvement at all. Therefore this Impoft doth now operate in the very Manner which every Tax ought, and every good one neceffarily will do: That is, it punifhes the Idle and the Sluggards for not improving their Eftates, but exempts the Diligent and Induftrious. Whereas in all other Countries throughout *Europe,* the Taxes upon Land annually rife or fall in Proportion to the Value or Produce: by which means the Proprietor is intimidated from improving his Eftate, leaft it fhould be burdened with an higher Tax the fucceeding Years.

MOREOVER, in regard to the Excife, many Branches thereof are very proper Taxes, and fit to be continued; thofe efpecially which are laid on intoxicating Liquors, or on Articles of Parade, Expence, and Pleafure. For, the further any Article is removed from the unavoidable Wants, and abfolute Neceffities of Life, the fitter it is to contribute towards the Support of the State by paying a Tax. And as to intoxicating Liquors, they are the fartheft removed of any whatever, and the moft detrimental to the State in their Effects and Confequences; therefore in every View, they are the propereft to have very high and difcouraging Duties laid on them.

As to the various Cuftoms or Duties on Goods imported, or exported, there is one certain Rule, whereby a Perfon of any moderate Capacity might judge with fufficient Exactnefs, whether fuch Cuftoms are right, *i. e.* properly laid on, or not; *viz.* Let him fuppofe the State to be a living Perfonage, ftanding on the Key of fome great Sea Port, and examining the Goods as loading,—or unloading. In the former Cafe, if the Goods to be exported, are completely manufactured, having undergone the full Induftry and Labour of his own People, he ought to lay no Embargo whatever upon them, but to fhew the Exporters all the Favour he can, and to protect them in that good Work. Whereas if the Goods are only manufactured in Part, or, what is worfe ftill, if they are abfolutely raw Materials, he fhould lay fuch Taxes upon them to check and difcourage their going out of the Kingdom in *that* Condition, as may be proportionate to their

unmanu-

unmanufactured, or raw-material State: That is, if they are absolutely raw Materials, they ought to have the highest Tax laid upon them, and in some Cases even such as may amount to a Prohibition. But if they are partly manufactured, and partly otherwise, the Tax should be lessened in Proportion as they recede from the State of raw Materials, and approach to complete Manufactures. —— In regard to Goods imported, his Conduct ought to be just the very reverse of the former; that is, he ought to lay the highest and most discouraging Taxes upon foreign *complete* Manufactures, in order to prevent their being worn or used in his Kingdom, —— a less discouraging upon others that are incomplete, —— and still less upon those that are but little removed from the raw-material State. As to raw Materials themselves, they ought to be admitted into every Port of the Kingdom, *Duty free*; unless there are some very peculiar Circumstances to create an Exception to this general Rule. Now the Grounds or Foundation of all this Reasoning, is——national Industry and Labour: Because these are the only Riches of a Kingdom. And therefore, if foreign Manufactures are to be discouraged by Taxes, least they should prevent the Labour of our own People; foreign intoxicating Liquors ought to be discouraged still more: —— Because they are not only to be considered under the Notion of complete Manufactures in their Kind, but such Manufactures likewise as take up the Time, and destroy the Industry of our own People in the using them. A Man may wear a Coat of *French* Cloth, and yet not lose an Hour in his proper Trade or Business; but he cannot lay out so much Money in *French* Wines or Brandies, without losing a great many.

THE last Article of Taxes is the Stamp Duties; and as some of them are very proper, and none of them amiss, we shall here conclude this Head of the Query with one short Reflection, *viz.* as that Tax which promotes Labour, and checks Idleness, is a very good one; so no others ought to be esteemed absolutely *bad*, but such only which produce the contrary Effect.

WHEREFORE, from this Observation, let us now pass on to consider, what Taxes ought to be repealed, according to the Principles here laid down.

IN the first Place, the Salt Tax can have no shadow of an Argument to plead in its behalf. For if Salt is a good Manure for Lands, the taxing of Salt is the taxing of Manure. And surely all Manures are raw Materials of the most important, most extensive Nature. Judge therefore, how impolitic it must be to stop so many Improvements,

ments,

ments, and the Circulation of fo much Labour, by one fingle Tax; which, according to the Nature of all bad Taxes, produces but very little into the Exchequer.   But further, Salt is an abfolute Neceffary of Life, adminiftering to no Pride, Vanity, or Excefs whatever, and confequently the moft improper to be taxed. — To illuftrate this by its Contraries; A Man who keeps a Coach, may expect to be refpected, and therefore deferves to be rated for it; becaufe a Coach is to be confidered as a Difplay of his Rank and Riches: But the Man who keeps a Salt-Box, only fhews the Neceffity he is under of preferving his Meat fweet and wholefome: And he is not efteemed by his Neighbours to be the greater, or richer Man upon that Account.   Once more, A Man may idle away a great deal of his Time in Taverns, drinking to the Prejudice of his Health, the Spending of his Subftance, ruining his Family, fubverfion of good Morals, and fetting a bad Example.   Therefore, fince intoxicating Liquors may, and often do produce thefe bad Effects, they are fit Subjects for Taxation.   But the Ufe of Salt is liable to none of thefe Evils; nor will the Man who waftes away Hours and Days together at his Bottle, keep his Saltfeller a Moment longer by him than he really wants it.   Why therefore fhould this ufeful raw Material, this Neceffary of Life, this harmlefs, inoffenfive Thing, incapable of Abufe, Vanity, Extravagance, or Excefs; — Why, in the Name of Common Senfe, fhould it be taxed?

2*dly*, The Duty on Coals is a very pernicious Duty; and fubject to all the Objections of the former; only fome of them in a leffer Degree.

3*dly*, The Duty on Soap and Candles is not a good Tax; and yet not wholly bad. — That Part which affects the Poor, or even the middling People, muft certainly be bad.   But the Soap and Candles ufed by the Great, in which the chief Confumption and Extravagance confift, ought to pay a Duty; and it would be really a Pity, that Beaux and Belles fhould not contribute fomething to the Support of Government, in Proportion as they frequented Balls, Affemblies, Operas, Plays, Mafquerades, Routs, Drums, &c. &c.   But in regard to the Poor, perhaps were the Duty on Candles fo conftituted, that only great Candles fhould pay, and the fmall ones, *viz.* thofe of twelve and upwards to the Pound be exempted; this would be a very ufeful Emendation. — As to the Duty on Soap, it is exceeding difficult to fuggeft any Amendments of this Nature, though it much wants it.   Yet, feeing that Drawbacks are allowed for all Soap and

Candles

Candles uſed in Manufactures, we muſt in Juſtice acknowledge, that the Effects of this Tax are not ſo prejudicial as many People are apt to imagine.

4*thly*, THE Duty on Leather is ſubject to ſome Objections, as it affects the Poor almoſt equally with the Rich. But yet of bad Taxes, it is far from being the worſt.

5*thly*, THE extravagant Duty upon the Importation of coarſe Olive Oil, a raw Material incapable either of Exceſs, Vanity, or Waſte of Time, and a moſt neceſſary Article for our Woollen Manufactures, and in making *Caſtile* Soap, is one that calls the loudeſt for Redreſs. And ſurely, after what hath been ſaid, it is needleſs to expatiate any more on the Impropriety or Abſurdity of ſuch a Tax. But there are two peculiar Circumſtances attending this Affair, which to many Perſons are but little known, and yet deſerve an eſpecial Conſideration. The one is, That our Sugar Iſlands, and Southern Colonies, where the Heat is ſo intenſe as to render *Tallow* Soap in a great Meaſure uſeleſs or offenſive, are under a Neceſſity of having *Oil* Soap from the *French*, and other Foreigners; becauſe the high Duties upon the Materials are a Diſcouragement to the making of ſuch Soap in *England*; and alſo becauſe the Drawback upon Exportation bears no Proportion to the Duty paid for the raw Materials on Importation. And if a Country is under a Neceſſity of taking *one* Manufacture, that one will introduce many more.——The other is, That when *Caſtile*, or Oil Soap is made in *England*, and uſed by the Clothier, he receives no greater a Drawback for it than if he had uſed Tallow Soap; whereas the Drawback upon foreign-made Soap is equal, or very nearly equal to the original Duty: So that, in Fact, according as Matters now ſtand, our own Manufacture is diſcouraged in both Reſpects, and that of Foreigners preferred.

AND having thus finiſhed the preſent Examination, it may not be improper to add, for the Credit of our Country, and Praiſe of the Legiſlature, that upon the moſt impartial Survey, there ſeem to be only theſe five Taxes of any Conſequence, which can ſtrictly be denominated *Bad*; and among theſe, the Duties on Salt, Coal, and coarſe Olive Oil are by much the worſt, and therefore ought to be the firſt repealed.——At leaſt the Duty on Oil, if not totally repealed [which perhaps would be objected to; becauſe, if Duty-free, it might come in ſo cheap as to ſuperſede the Uſe of Train, or Fiſh Oil] ſhould nevertheleſs be conſiderably leſſened, and reduced from 6*l.* 3*s.* 2*d. per* Ton, the preſent Rate, to 30*s.* or 40*s. per* Ton.

BUT

But after having ſpecified the bad Taxes, will it be amiſs, or can it be judged unſeaſonable to ſuggeſt *one* great Improvement eaſily to be made in ſome of the good ones? *viz.* In regard to the Cuſtoms, To permit (though not oblige) the Merchants to land their Goods without prompt Payment of Duties at the Cuſtom-houſe? — Were this Permiſſion granted, thoſe who accepted of it ſhould be obliged to give Bond for the Payment, and to put their Goods under the Lock and Key of the Officer, by way of additional Security. And then they ſhould be allowed to diſpoſe of their Effects, and to pay the Duties gradually; according as they could find Purchaſers, or as they wanted to remove ſuch or ſuch particular Parcels, Hogſheads, Butts, Pipes, &c. out of the public, to their own private Warehouſes. By theſe Means, every Merchant could extend his Trade and Credit to an infinitely greater Degree than he can do at preſent; becauſe he would need to make no Reſerves of Caſh or Credit for prompt Payments at the Cuſtom-houſe; every Merchant alſo could buy when, and where, and as much as he pleaſed on Speculation; and ſuſtain no Loſs of Intereſt of that Money, which muſt be *now* advanced to pay the Duties; and which Intereſt, even in the Caſe of Drawbacks, upon the preſent Footing, never is, and never can be returned.—Becauſe, though the Duty is returned, the Intereſt of the Money paid for it ſtill remains unreturned, a great Loſs to the Merchant, yet no Gains to the Government. — In ſhort, this ſingle Regulation would go a great Way towards making *Great Britain* a Magazine and Store-houſe for other Countries, and render all her Ports FREE.

Q. What new Taxes ought to be laid on, according to the preſent Doctrine of preventing Idleneſs, promoting Induſtry, and checking Extravagance?

A. Taxes ought to be laid on Dogs, on Saddle-Horſes, when exceeding two in Number; on Livery Servants, on all Places of public Reſort and Diverſion, ſuch as public Rooms, Muſic-Gardens, Play-Houſes, &c. alſo on Booths and Stands for Country Wakes, Cricket Matches, and Horſe Racing, Stages for Mountebanks, Cudgel Playing, &c. moreover on Fives Places, and Ball Courts, Billiard Tables, Shuffle Boards, Skittle Alleys, Bowling Greens, and Cock Pits: — Alſo Capitation Taxes ſhould be levied on itinerant Players, Lottery-men, Shew-men, Jugglers, Ballad Singers, and indeed on all others of whatever Claſs or Denomination, whoſe very Trades and Profeſſions have a natural Tendency, and whoſe perſonal Intereſt it is to make other People profuſe, extravagant, and idle. Laſtly,

The

The Stamp Duty might very properly be extended to take in printed Songs, Novels, Romances, Mufic, Plays, and fuch like Articles of mere Amufement, to be ftampt in the fame Manner as Almanacks are. — Now it is obvious, that fuch Taxes as thefe are fo far from impoverifhing, that they muft neceffarily enrich every State where they take Place. And therefore, let it be laid down as an infallible Rule, that in Proportion as this Syftem of Taxation, or its Contrary, doth prevail in any State throughout the World, in the fame Proportion doth Induftry or Idlenefs, Plenty or Want, Riches or Beggary prevail likewife. For in fhort, the Courfe of Nature is fixed, and cannot be altered. What have we then to do but to endeavour to accommodate ourfelves to the invariable Rules of Divine Providence; and not foolifhly expect, that Wrong fhould be made Right, or the Crooked be pronounced Straight to pleafe Us?

Queries relating to the Spirit and Effence of the Conftitution.

Q. WHAT is the general Refult of the *prefent English* Conftitution, confidered as operating upon the Minds of the People, and producing certain, diftinguifhing Effects in their Conduct and Behaviour?

A. THE general Refult is — An Independence of the lower and middling People in regard to the Great, — but a Dependence of the Great upon them. And from the Clafhing or Mixture of thefe two oppofite Principles, arifes that medley, or Contradiction of Characters fo remarkable in the *English* Nation. The People are independent, becaufe they have nothing to fear, and very little to hope from the Power of the Great; but the Great are rendered dependent upon them; becaufe, without the Affiftance or Approbation of the People, they cannot be confiderable either in the Senate, or out of it; they cannot either be Minifters themfelves, or raife an effectual Oppofition to the Miniftry of others. Hence it is, that the Bulk of the People are always appealed to in every Difpute; and being thus erected into fovereign Arbitrators, they act without Difguife, and indeed without Referve; fo that both the good and bad Qualities in human Nature, appear bolder and more prominent in the Inhabitants of *England,* than in thofe of any other Country. For if the People are good, they are remarkably fo; but if they are bad, they will take no Pains to conceal their Vices. Their unbounded Generofity, Franknefs of Difpofition, great Sincerity, and above all, their glowing Spirit of Patriotifm, are Proofs of the former; and the Surlinefs, Brutality, and daring, declared Venality and Proftitution of many among them,

are

are too sad Instances of the latter. In other Countries, the Mass of the People know nothing of State Affairs ; being Things indeed dangerous to be meddled with : And therefore they are simple and credulous, believing what is told them, and inquiring no farther.—But in *England*, every Creature is a Politician ; and has formed in his own Mind the best System both for Peace and War. He dislikes the Ministry, because he is no Minister himself ; and therefore reckons up all their Failings, and a great many more than ever belonged to them : and if Things go on unsuccessfully, he is sure to impute it to the Fault, rather than the Misfortune of the Administration ; because it is natural to a free People to be suspicious of their Governors ; but he never distrusts his own Opinion, or imagines another may see farther, or know better than himself. Thus it is, that the *English* Populace are too deeply versed in Politics, — and yet too little ; too deeply to obey with Readiness and Chearfulness ; and too little, to make a wise and prudent Choice for themselves. On the other Hand, the Great, finding no other Way to the Honours and Emoluments of the State, and the Gratification of their Ambition, but through the Labyrinths of Popularity, take the shortest and the surest Road they can find, to arrive at them ; that is, they apply to the Passions and Foibles of the People, rather than inform their Reason, or enlighten their Judgments. For the Mass of Mankind are much sooner cajoled, than instructed. Flattery is pleasing, Instruction disagreeable and forbidding. Therefore a Candidate at an Election, is servile and fawning to an astonishing Degree : He consults the Humours, Tempers, Caprices, Follies, nay, the Vices of the voting Mob, their Friends and Acquaintance ; and suits his own Behaviour accordingly. Nothing is too abject for him to stoop to, no Lye so absurd, no party Distinction so ridiculous, that he will not by himself, or his Agents, make use of on that Occasion. And while the mental Part of these unhappy People is thus continually inflamed with Noise and Nonsense ; their brutal and animal Part is gorged and intoxicated with Gluttony and Drunkenness. — But if the Candidate is out-done by his Antagonist in these *disguised* Methods of Bribery and Corruption ; if he is inferior to the other in the Arts of political Lying, popular Declamation, Carousing, and Huzzaing ; then he has Recourse, as the last Shift, to the tempting Influence of pecuniary Bribes ; and so corrupts the Heart, where he cannot corrupt the Understanding. Thus it is, that many of the Nobility and Gentry in *England* are too frequently found to have certain Meannesses neffes and Bafeneffes in their Conduct, which are feldom to be met with in other Countries among Perfons of the fame elevated Rank, and Station. And yet, as a great deal muft ftill depend upon the Reputation of a good Character, and as it is impoffible, that popular Deception fhould laft long, or ferve in all Cafes; the very fame Motives of Popularity, which lead them to do much Evil in fome Inftances, operate as powerfully towards doing great Good in others. Hence that diffufive Charity, great Liberality, and Condefcenfion, fo confpicuous in Perfons of Fortune in this Country; hence thofe noble Inftances of public Beneficence for the Relief of the Poor, in Times of Scarcity and general Diftrefs; hence alfo that Rivalfhip and Emulation in fome of the Members of the Legiflature, to patronize a public-fpirited Scheme, and to take the Lead in doing the moft fignal Service to their Country. In fhort, this Independency, and this Dependency create fuch a Mixture of good and bad Effects, both in the inferior, and fuperior Stations, that it is difficult to fay which of them at prefent do preponderate, and whether the Balance at the Foot of the Account can be placed to the doing more Benefit, or more Harm to Society. — But it is to be hoped and earneftly wifhed, that fome Method or other may be happily hit upon to produce the fame, or more Good, and yet avoid the Evil.

Q. If the Conftitution hath this univerfal, and almoft irrefiftible Influence on all Ranks and Conditions of Life, What is the Confequence in regard to certain Profeffions, Trades, and Stations? And hath it rendered fome of them more, or lefs honourable and eligible than others?

A. As the Spirit and Bent of the Conftitution fo ftrongly point towards Liberty and Independency, the Confequence is, that every Profeffion or Occupation is deemed honourable or eligible in Proportion as it can attain this great End. And hence it is, that the Military Service, fo much coveted in other Countries, as the moft honourable, is not entitled to very great Refpects in this; *viz.* becaufe it creates a Dependency, inftead of promoting an Independency; hence alfo the true Reafon, why Trades, even mechanic Trades, are no Difgrace, provided they produce Riches; becaufe Riches in every free Country neceffarily make the Poffeffors independent. In *England,* an Haberdafher in his Coach, is certainly as much confidered as a Captain in his Scarlet; and if he fhould happen to be a Member of Parliament, which is no impoffible Cafe, the Military Man would be much more likely to fue to him for Favour with the Miniftry,

than

than he to the other. Thus therefore, as Wealth creates Independency, fo it is, for the moft Part, that Trades and Profeffions are rated and valued in Proportion as they produce Wealth. Why elfe is the Brewer preferable to the Baker, or the Pin-maker to the Butcher? There may indeed be fome Exceptions to this general Rule: but they are fo few, as not to deferve a diftinct Confideration. And certain it is, that though the low bred Mechanic may not always meet with Refpect equal to his large acquired Fortune; yet, if he gives his Son a liberal and accomplifhed Education, — the Birth and Calling of the Father are funk in the Son; and the Son is reputed, if his Carriage is fuitable, a Gentleman in all Companies, though without ferving in the Army, without Patent, Pedigree, or Creation. In one Word, Trade begets Wealth, and Wealth Independence: But the Affiftance of Learning and Education muft be called in, in order to fet off, and embellifh them both. Thus therefore it cometh to pafs, that a competent Share of Wealth, Learning, and improved Senfe, is more generally diffufed throughout all Orders and Degrees of Men in this Country, than perhaps in any other: And the different Stations of Life fo run into, and mix with each other, that it is hard to fay, where the one ends, and the other begins. — In other Countries it is not fo.

Q. Are the *Englifh* Nobility and Gentry more difpofed to Town Refidences than Country ones, or *vice verfa?* And what Effects doth the Spirit of the Conftitution feem to produce in regard to either, or both thefe Things?

A. Were the prefent Conftitution removed, or altered, perhaps a Town Refidence would be the chief Delight: But as Matters now ftand, the Conftitution ftrongly, though filently difpofes them to chufe both in their refpective Seafons. To explain this, let it be obferved that a Country Refidence is neceffary in order to create a Country Intereft: For, was the great Man never to fee, to converfe with, or refide among his Country Neighbours (I mean the Neighbours to his Country Eftate) he would foon find, that another of much lefs Property, would eclipfe him in Influence and Power; and that the independent *Britons* would give their Votes to that Candidate who ftudied moft to pleafe them. Hence therefore a kind of conftitutional Neceffity is formed of refiding at leaft fome Time in the Country; and fince a Refidence for fome Part of the Year or other muft be chofe, a Summer Refidence is certainly the moft agreeable. [Not to mention, that in the Winter, the very fame Conftitution calls them up to Parliament.] But when Perfons are once habituated to a

Thing,

Thing, they take a liking to it, and feem to prefer it to another. Therefore a Country Seat becomes a Matter of Choice; and as fuch, is ornamented and improved, till at length it doth an Honour to the Owner, and raifes the Emulation of others. Then the Example fpreads and catches; and Building and Planting become a Fafhion. Thus it is, that the Country Seats of the *Englifh*, their Parks and Woods, their Gardens, Plantations, Fifh-Ponds, and Canals are infinitely more numerous, more beautiful, and formed upon a better Plan, and kept in neater Order (having more Care, as well as Expence beftowed upon them) than are ufual in other Countries. But, were it ever to come to pafs, that the Parliament fhould chufe their own Members, by filling up Vacancies as they happened; — this one Circumftance would caufe a total Revolution; and the whole Tafte for Country Improvements, rural Decorations, and Summer Refidences, would be foon at an End; *viz.* Becaufe the great Families would then refide wholly at the Capital, as they do in other Countries; or elfe they would refort to Places of public Diverfions, Baths, Mineral Waters, *&c.* inftead of cultivating an Acquaintance with their Country Neighbours. This therefore is a ftriking Inftance of the Power and Influence of the prefent Conftitution.—An Influence, which operates much ftronger than any pofitive Law whatever. For were this Conftitution, obliging to Country Refidences, altered or deftroyed, you might make a thoufand Penal Laws for the keeping up of the Country Seats, embellifhing of Parks, Gardens, Canals, *&c.* and yet without Effect; becaufe they would foon be forgot and difregarded. But when a Polity of this Nature is once formed, and fet a going, it proceeds on of itfelf, requiring neither Judge nor Jury, Plantiff nor Informer, to enforce its Execution.

RELIGIOUS CAUSES.

2. WHAT are the moral and focial Effects, which the Religion publicly profeffed in *England*, hath a natural Tendency to produce?

A. IN regard to Society, as this is the only View in which the Religion publicly profeffed, is to be here confidered, it may not be amifs to give an *authorized*, and therefore an unexceptionable Account of its Nature and Tendency; *viz.* " It teaches us to love our Neigh-
" bours as ourfelves, —and to do to all as we would they fhould do
" to us,—to love, honour, and fuccour our Parents,—to honour
" and obey the King, and all that are put in Authority under him,
" —to fubmit ourfelves to all our Governors, Teachers, Spiritual
" Paftors,

" Paftors, and Mafters,——to order ourfelves lowly and reverently to
" our Betters,——to hurt no Body by Word or Deed,——to be true
" and juft in all our Dealings,——to bear no Malice or Hatred in our
" Hearts,——to keep our Hands from Picking and Stealing,——our
" Tongues from Evil-fpeaking, Lying, and Slandering,——to keep
" our Bodies in Temperance, Soberness, and Chaftity,——not to covet
" or defire other Mens Goods,——but to learn and labour truly to get
" our own Living,——and to do our Duty in that State of Life unto
" which it fhall pleafe God to call us."

Now from the above Account, it is eafy to deduce one plain In-
ference; *viz.* That the Rules of Religion, and the Rules of focial Induftry do perfectly harmonize; and that all Things hurtful to the
latter, are indeed a Violation of the former. In fhort, the fame
good Being who formed the Religious Syftem, formed alfo the Commercial; and the End of both, as defigned by Providence, is no
other than this, That private Intereft fhould coincide with public,
felf with focial, and the prefent with future Happinefs. Thofe Men
therefore, who would reprefent the Principles of Religion, and the
Principles of Commerce as at Variance with each other, are in reality
Friends to neither.

2. HATH the Civil Conftitution unhappily eftablifhed any Circumftances in the State, which *eventually* counteract the natural good
Tendency of Religion? And if it hath, how might they be removed
or altered?

A. THERE are feveral Circumftances eftablifhed, which almoft
neceffarily introduce bad Morals; but the two Principal, and fuch as
are chargeable altogether upon the Conftitution, are Electioneering,
and the Frequency of Oaths. With regard to the former, fo much
hath been faid already, that it is become a very needlefs, as well as a
difagreeable Tafk to repeat it. Let us therefore, having feen too much
of this loathfome Difeafe, endeavour to find out a Cure. —— Or if not
a total Cure, at leaft a confiderable Remedy: And fuch, I think, is
not difficult to difcover. *Viz.* Let the Qualifications for Voting be
put upon fuch a Footing as would exclude, for the moft Part, the Idle,
Extravagant, and Debauched, but include and encourage the Sober,
Virtuous, and Ingenious: That is, Let Voting excite an Emulation
in Virtue, Induftry, and Sobriety, not in Vice, Intemperance, and
Debauchery. Now this would be greatly effected by fixing the Qualification both of a Freeholder, and a Burgefs, upon one fimple, equal
Plan, throughout the Kingdom; *viz.* Let that Eftate which is rated

for

for ten Pounds a Year or upwards to the Land-Tax, be the Qualification of Voting for a Freeholder :—And that Dwelling-house, if occupied wholly by a Man's self, and not let out to Lodgers, or In-Tenants,—that Dwelling-house, I say, in a Borough or City, which likewise pays to the Land-Tax after the Rate of ten Pounds a Year or upwards, be the Qualification of Voting as a Citizen or Burgess; and then, when these are fixed and settled, let all other Qualifications, Freedoms, Liberties, and exclusive Privileges be for ever abolished and destroyed.

Now were this the Case, waving all Commercial Views, the moral good Consequences would be exceeding great and extensive; And public Elections would in some Sense be Incitements to Virtue, instead of being, what they notoriously are at present, the Seminaries and Nurseries of Vice. Moreover, the Liberties of the People would be as well secured as ever; nay, much better, because they would be founded on superior Wisdom and Knowledge, and on undoubted Substance, and real Property; instead of that which is too much at present the Basis of popular Power; *viz.* Rags and Vermin, Noise and Nonsense. In short, nothing would suffer by this proposed Alteration; nothing would be demolished or diminished but Idleness, Drunkenness, and Extravagance; Lying, Swearing, and Forswearing; the Meanness of Superiors, and Insolence of Inferiors; Confusion, and every evil Work. And truly these are Things which might be parted with without Regret.

As to the Frequency of Oaths, were the Arch-Fiend himself, the grand Enemy of Mankind, to have studied all means possible towards annihilating the good Impressions of Religion, he could not have devised a more effectual Method than this, which is here ready contrived for him; there being scarce a considerable Branch of Duty either towards God or Man, but what is directly counter-acted by these Institutions. In regard to God, the Idea of Him as an Omnipresent Judge and Almighty Avenger, is obliterated and lost by the frequent Appeals made to Him, in such Cases, where the Subject-Matter is either amazingly low and trifling, or excessively improper.—Trifling surely would many Things appear, were one to give a formal Detail of all the absurd, or insignificant Passages, which might be collected out of the Statutes of Colleges and Universities,—out of the Customs, Charters, and By-Laws of Cities, Boroughs, Corporate Companies, and Legal Societies;—or even out of the public Statutes of the Realm. And yet, young Gentlemen at their Admission into

the

the Univerfity, Election upon Foundations, or taking of Degrees;
—alfo all Citizens or Burgeffes either upon receiving their Freedoms,
Admittance unto the Exercife of certain Trades, or ferving of Offices
in exclufive Companies,—and in fhort, Civil Magiftrates of every
Denomination, are refpectively fworn to obferve and enforce thefe
Articles, according to their Rank, and Station. It is not therefore,
—indeed it is not for want of Inftances, that I here forbear to produce the particular Paffages referred to; but becaufe the Subject itfelf is too ferious to be laughed at; being fitter to excite Horror,
than Ridicule.

As to *improper Occafions*, what fhall we think of fuch Oaths, which
either, in a Manner, require *Impoffibilities?* or *unneceffarily* lay the
Mind and Confcience under the moft diftrefsful Difficulties? And
yet thoufands, and hundreds of thoufands of fuch Oaths are confti-
tutionally impofed every Year. This is a Fact, which alas! there is
no Neceffity of proving; becaufe thofe, who are obliged to ferve the
Offices of Churchwardens, Conftables, &c. &c. and thofe who muft
tranfact Bufinefs in the feveral Branches of the Revenue, efpecially
the Excife, the Salt, and the Cuftoms, know it already but too well:
And as to others, whofe Scenes of Life lead them not into this fatal
Knowledge, there is no need of drawing them out of their happy
State of Ignorance.

But if the Duty towards God is thus intrenched upon, by fuch
a Multiplication of ufelefs, or improper Oaths; the Duty towards
Man is not lefs affected by the malignant Tendency of many of them.
And by this I do not mean to fay, that the Obligations to focial Virtue, Juftice, Honefty, and Integrity are neceffarily relaxed in Proportion as the firft Principle of Religion, *viz.* the Idea of an Omni-
prefent Judge, and Almighty Avenger, is become lefs awful and
affecting (though furely this itfelf is a moft alarming Confideration.)
But what is here intended is, that the exprefs Tenor, and almoft the
very Words of many of thefe Oaths are altogether repugnant to the
Duties of univerfal Benevolence and Good-will; and that a Man
cannot poffibly obferve *them,* and at the fame Time obferve the
Chriftian Maxim of — Doing as he would be done by. For Example, if the Concealments of Fraud and Iniquity, under the fpecious
Title of the MYSTERIES OF TRADE; and if the groffeft Difingenuity,
and fuch felfifh, fordid Views as are diametrically oppofite to the
Public Good, are to be enforced by the Sanction of an Oath, as
moft undoubtedly they daily are;—What confiderable Affiftance

can

can We expect from Religion, when it is thus imployed to deſtroy itſelf ? And if the Light that is in Us, is thus turned into Darkneſs, How great muſt that Darkneſs be ? In ſhort, were all the ſeveral Inſtances to be enumerated, wherein the natural Efficacy of Religion is unhappily counter-acted by ſome poſitive Civil Inſtitution ; it would perhaps appear a greater Wonder, that Religion, under ſuch Circumſtances, ſhould produce any good Effects at all, than that it ſhould produce ſo few.

But yet, theſe Evils, great and crying as they are, may moſt eaſily be removed, if heartily and ſincerely ſet about. And what is better ſtill, there is hardly a Poſſibility that any bad Conſequences ſhould attend the Alteration; for in ſuch a Caſe, no Mobs, no Inſurrections, nor even popular Clamours could be raiſed to oppoſe the Reformation ; no Struggles for Power, or Convulſions in the State could be excited ; nor any Proſpect of a Change in the Syſtem of Religion, or Government could, in Conſequence thereof, be wiſhed for by ſome, or feared by others. And now, ſhould you aſk, What is the Remedy propoſed, that can be ſo ſafely adminiſtered, and yet be adequate to ſo great an Evil ? The Anſwer is plainly this ; let all common or private Subjects, who are not called to *eſpecial Engagements* of Truſt or Fidelity in the Diſcharge of ſome particular Offices, or in Accounting with the Revenue, be ſuffered to live quietly under the Laws of the reſpective Societies to which they belong, without previouſly requiring any expreſs Covenant whatever : — But let every other Perſon, who is more immediately called to ſome particular Engagement, be expreſſly obliged, under large Bonds and Penalties, beſides the uſual legal Puniſhments, to diſcharge it faithfully. And thus, by theſe two ſimple, eaſy Reformations, at leaſt a Million of Perjuries would be prevented every Year. For by the firſt, all Students in the Univerſities, Citizens, Burgeſſes, Freemen of Trading Companies, Voters at Elections, &c. &c. would be left free from the horrid Abuſe and Entanglement of Oaths ; and yet be as much under the Command, *Juriſdiction*, and *Puniſhment* of their reſpective Laws, as they are at preſent : And in regard to the ſecond, all Civil Magiſtrates, from the higheſt to the loweſt Order ; all Officers in the Revenue, Merchants, Captains of Ships, Tanners, Tea-Sellers, &c. &c. would thereby be diſcharged from ſuch Oaths, which, as Matters now ſtand, are in many Reſpects impoſſible to be kept, and in others are but little, very little obſerved, when found to interfere with immediate Intereſt and preſent Profit : — Yet, though theſe ſeveral Claſſes

of

of People would be diſcharged from Oaths, they would ſtill remain under the Obligation of Bonds, Penalties, and legal Puniſhments; nay, be liable to higher Bonds and Penalties, than at preſent they are ſubject to. This being the Caſe, What further Securities are to be given, or can you require? — Indeed, let me aſk, What are the preſent Securities (ſuch I mean, on which any Streſs or Confidence is put) were you to ſuppoſe all Bonds, Penalties, and legal Puniſhments to be totally ſet aſide? As to the Multiplicity of Oaths, ſo frequently taken; that theſe are not looked upon as any real Security, is evident from hence; *viz.* every Merchant, or Maſter of a Veſſel who ſwears to his Import at the Cuſtom-houſe, hath his Goods as much watched and guarded by the Officers, as if they did not believe one Word which he had ſworn. Why therefore is he compelled to ſwear at all, ſince his Swearing produces no Sort of Confidence, and gives no Satisfaction whatever to the Impoſer of the Oath? In one Word, let daily Experience determine this Affair.— We have, for Example, a prodigious Multitude of Imployments now in the Kingdom; all which may be termed *Offices* or *Places* in a general Senſe, with no great Impropriety: That is, they may be ſtiled Poſts of Honour, or Profit, or perhaps both; Poſts of Truſt, or Gain, or probably of both united. This being the Caſe, I ſhall, for the Sake of greater Diſtinction, beg Leave to divide them into two Claſſes; *viz.* Thoſe of the *new,*—and thoſe of the *old* Creation. The Offices of the New Creation, are ſuch as have partly ariſen, and partly been inſtituted ſince the Reformation; and will be found to conſiſt chiefly of Gorvernorſhips, Guardianſhips, Treaſureſhips, and Truſteeſhips in the Management of Schools, Hoſpitals, Almshouſes, Infirmaries, and many other Foundations of late Erection: To theſe may be likewiſe added the Maſterſhips, and Uſherſhips of Schools; the Places of Phyſicians, Surgeons, Apothecaries, Matrons, and Nurſes in Hoſpitals and Infirmaries; alſo all Imployments ariſing from mercantile Commiſſions, Agencies, Factorages, Partnerſhips, Purſerſhips, and the like; not to mention thoſe belonging to Compting-houſes, Store-houſes, Magazines, Bankers-ſhops, and many others. Be it therefore ſufficient to obſerve, that all theſe Imployments (call them Offices, or otherwiſe it matters not;) yet all are attended with a conſiderable Share either of Honour, or Profit according to their reſpective Natures; and that ſome of them are among the moſt important, and others the moſt lucrative Stations in the whole Kingdom; requiring the greateſt Degree of Diligence, and

Integrity

Integrity in their Difcharge and Execution. Yet, great, important, and lucrative as many of them are, you can hardly fay, that a fingle Oath of Admiffion is required in any one of them. This is a ftriking Circumftance, and highly deferves the public Attention. —— On the contrary, The Offices of the Old Creation, are all the Parts of Government, of Civil Magiftracy, and of the Revenue from the higheft to the loweft; alfo the feveral Mafterfhips, Wardenfhips, Treafurefhips, &c. of Corporations, and Companies of Trades; and indeed of almoft every other Charter, and Foundation, Civil, Commercial, or Religious, if granted, or eftablifhed prior to the Reformation. Now in regard to the Admiffion into each of thefe, the Reader is defired to take efpecial Notice, that the Solemnity of an Oath is required over and over, even though the Subject-Matter to which it relates, fhould be of no more Importance than the Office of a Scavenger. This being the Cafe, and thefe the Diftinctions between the Offices of the Old, and of the New Creation, permit me to afk this one Queftion, *viz.* In what Refpects are the Swearers obferved to difcharge their refpective Duties, better than the Non-Swearers? or did you ever difcover, that the Adminiftering fo many Oaths was attended with any folid Advantage in the one Cafe; or the Non-Adminiftering with any real Difadvantage in the other? Nay, to go farther; were your own Clerk, Steward, Bailiff, Butler, Groom, Houfe-keeper, and all the menial Servants in your Houfe now to take ever fo many Oaths, that they would behave with Honefty, Diligence, Fidelity, and Sobriety in your Service; —— Would you repofe one Jot the more Confidence in them upon that Account? No; I am certain, you would not. Why therefore fhould fuch Oaths be continued any longer in *fimilar Cafes*; feeing it hath been made out as clear as the Sun, that they ferve to no other Purpofe in the World, but to involve Thoufands and Millions in the Guilt of Perjury?

But the Origin of thefe Oaths is a farther Reafon why they fhould be now abolifhed: Of which take the following brief Relation: *viz.* When the Tyranny and Wickednefs of Popery prevailed, the Priefts invented and recommended the Ufe of Oaths upon almoft every Occafion. This they did under a Pretence of mixing the Duties of Religion with the Affairs of Civil Life; but with a real View of extending their Empire of auricular Confeffion, and thereby of bringing the Laity under the Neceffity of applying to *them* for Pardon, and purchafing Abfolution. And the Defign thus deeply laid, fucceeded to their Wifhes for many Ages. But as the Reformation came on, the Doctrine of

auricular

auricular Confeſſion, and judicial Abſolution ſunk and died away: Yet in the Hurry and Confuſion of the Times, ſome of thoſe very Corruptions, which made auricular Confeſſion appear neceſſary, or at leaſt plauſible, were over-looked and forgot: So that the ſhameful Frequency, and improper Uſe of Oaths not only continued, in the Inſtances above related, but even gained Ground in after Times, to the particular Diſgrace of this Proteſtant State and Nation. And thus is too fully verified that Remark, frequently repeated in *The Elements of Commerce, viz.* That we ſtill remain in the Dregs of Popery, in regard to certain Points of Practice, tho' we have fully abjured thoſe Principles, on which ſuch corrupt Practices were originally built. Indeed the pious and well-meaning Father *Queſnel* honeſtly endeavoured to reform theſe Abuſes, even in the Church of *Rome*; ſetting forth the Unreaſonableneſs and Wickedneſs of continuing ſuch Oaths, and the Dangers thence ariſing to the Souls of Men. But alas! this very Poſition, which certainly hath not a Spark of Hereſy, or Enthuſiaſm belonging to it (whatever ſome other Parts of his Works might have) was condemned by the Pope in the hundred and firſt Propoſition of the famous Bull *Unigenitus*, as heretical, ill-ſounding, and offenſive to Catholic Tradition. — Thus far as to the Hiſtorical Account of the Riſe and Progreſs of the Evil here complained of.—And now let me be permitted to cloſe the Whole with this one Reflection; *viz.* That tho' the Pope may condemn any Attempts towards the Diſcontinuance of unneceſſary or improper Oaths, through Motives beſt known to himſelf; yet the Senſe of Reaſon and Revelation is evidently this, *viz.* That Swearing, or a ſolemn Appeal to the Court of Heaven ſhould be the laſt Reſource of all; and only to be uſed on the moſt important Occaſions, and where other Methods cannot ſucceed. Therefore in Proportion as you deviate from this Rule, you proſtitute one of the moſt ſacred Ordinances of Religion; you counter-act its Deſign, and make Religion become a Parricide to itſelf; you looſen the Bands of human Society; and in every Reſpect you take *the Name of God in vain.*

Q. Doth the Religion by Law eſtabliſhed allow a Toleration to thoſe Perſons, whoſe Conſciences will not permit them to join in its Worſhip and Communion?

A. The Principles of the Proteſtant Religion being founded in the Right of private Judgment (for our firſt Reformers had no other Right to juſtify their Separation from the Church of *Rome*) it evidently follows, that all Proteſtants, if they will act conſiſtently, muſt

allow

allow that Right to others, which they claim themselves. And yet, clear as this Proposition now appears, its Evidence was not seen, at least not acknowledged by Protestants of *any* Denomination whatever, till a great many Years after the Reformation. So difficult a Thing it is for the Light of Truth to make its Way, where the Minds of Men have been long wrapped up in Darkness: — And herein we must ingenuously confess,

Illiacos intra muros peccatur, & extra.

THE *Dutch* were the first People, who caused the Doctrine of a Toleration to be incorporated into their Civil Constitution: And yet, it is much to be queried, whether their true Motives had not more of the Commercial, than Religious Merit belonging to them. But be that as it may, this Doctrine was certainly adopted here in *England* upon Motives of Conscience, at the Time of the happy Revolution; and seems now so firmly rooted in the Judgments of the whole Kingdom; that scarce a Person can be found to oppose it openly. Nay, were any Author to assert, at this Time of Day, that three or four hundred Thousand Persons ought to be imprisoned, or expelled the Realm, or otherwise persecuted; rather than be permitted to live in a Non-conformity to the Established Church; he would meet with that universal Contempt and Indignation, he had so justly deserved. And as to the Church of *England* itself, What is the Consequence of this Lenity and Indulgence? Why truly, the Effects are so far from being prejudicial to her, that they strengthen her Interests every Day: And in Proportion as the former Heats and Animosities subside, in the same Proportion do Men seem better disposed to join in her Worship and Communion. Indeed some few prejudiced Persons, perhaps naturally of a malevolent Temper, may still remain on both Sides, who would be for reviving the former Contentions: But they are in all Respects so very inconsiderable, as to merit no Share of the Public Regard. If any Competition is now subsisting, it is of a much nobler Kind, *viz.* Which Side, the Church, or the Dissenting, shall have the Honour of producing the most eminent Persons in all Branches of useful Learning, particularly the Knowledge of the Scriptures. And Competitions of this Sort, will never do any Mischief to either Church, or State.

Q. DOTH the Religion of the Country create a great Number of idle Holidays, and pompous Processions? And what are the Consequences regarding both the Industry, and Morals of the People?

A. AN

A. An *Englishman*, who is to travel into foreign Countries, muſt ſee the Propriety of inſerting theſe Queſtions in a Treatiſe of this Nature : Though as far as regards his own Country and Religion, thanks to the happy Reformation, they are become unneceſſary and ſuperfluous.

Q. Doth the Religion of the Country injoin a long and ſevere Lent, requiring its People to conform ſtrictly to a Fiſh-Diet, as a meritorious Act of Piety towards God? If ſo, — What Exceſſes of Gluttony and Gormandizing are obſervable, either at the Approach, or after the Concluſion of this extraordinary Seaſon? And what Diſeaſes or Diſtempers are diſcoverable, as proceeding from ſuch a ſudden and unnatural Change both of the Quality, and Quantity of the uſual Food.

A. The preſent Reply to this Queſtion muſt be the ſame as the former.

Q. Doth the Religion of the Country inculcate Celibacy, and recommend a Solitary, or monaſtic Life as the moſt meritorious; inſtead of giving the Preference to the Active, Induſtrious, and the Social? Moreover, are there any Orders of Religious Beggars to be found? and are ſuch Inſtitutions to be imputed to the avowed Principles of the Religion of the Country?

A. Alike Anſwer to be returned, as before.

Q. What public Proviſions are made either by the Religious, or Civil Inſtitutions of the Country towards the proper Training up of Youth in the Principles of Religion and Virtue? And are there any Parochial Liſts annually required to be given in, of ſuch young Perſons, as having been inſtructed during the preceding Year, are capable of giving a ſufficient Account of thoſe Duties, which conſtitute the good Chriſtian, — and the good Citizen?

A. The Eccleſiaſtical Eſtabliſhment hath done tolerably well; but the Civil having done nothing at all in this Reſpect, the Conſequence is, That every Effort of the Religious Part of the Conſtitution becomes fruitleſs and vain. The Methods of public Inſtruction propoſed by the Church, are Catechiſing on Sundays in the Afternoon; which Methods are undoubtedly good in themſelves, and would certainly ſoon produce a viſible Reformation, were they properly attended. But the Misfortune is, That as Catechiſing is an Application to the Judgment, and not to the Paſſions of Mankind; it is deſtitute of thoſe Charms which draw Numbers together, whether of young or old. For as it hath nothing belonging to it, to capti-
vate

vate either the Eyes of the Spectators, or the Ears of the Audience;
and as it is neither of the Comedy, nor Tragedy kind, its Influence
on an independent [not to fay, a *licentious*] People, is juft as much
as they pleafe themfelves:—which is almoft juft nothing at all.
This is a Fact, which the Author of thefe Sheets is forry to fay, he
can too well atteft upon the Experience of many Years. Add to
this, that the Rich will not fcruple to declare, That they do not chufe
to fend their Children to mix with the Poor, leaft they fhould be in-
jured in their Morals by contracting Acquaintance with them, (not
to mention other Reafons, which perhaps have their Foundation in
Pride and Vanity): And as to the Poor, thofe few among them,
who are difpofed to fend their Offspring to be inftructed, think it
very fufficient to oblige them to attend at fuch a Period of Child-
hood, when they are fitter for the alphabetical Rudiments of the
School-miftrefs, than the rational Inftructions of the Paftor. In
fhort, the propereft Seafons for Catechifing are thofe, when the
Underftanding is opened, and the Paffions are on the Wing in pur-
fuit of Objects. For if you begin fooner, you inftruct the Parrot,
and not the Man: But alas, if you defer it to the proper Time, and
expect that Youth fhould the more conftantly attend, in Proportion
as they advance towards Maturity, you will find, that thofe of the
better Sort efteem themfelves above it, and thofe of the inferior judge
themfelves paft it:—And in both thefe unhappy Prejudices, they
are too much abetted by their refpective Parents. This being the
Cafe, the Religious Part of our Conftitution cannot be blamed, if
fo little Good is effected; becaufe it is impoffible to go to the Root
of the Evil, unlefs the temporal Power will lend fome Affiftance.
Were indeed fome Civil Polity eftablifhed in order to enforce the
Bufinefs of Catechifing both on the Catechift, and Catechumen; (and
fuch might eafily be devifed, without making any Intrufions on
Liberty of Confcience) a confiderable Good might be effected. Or
rather were the parochial Paftors univerfally obliged to deliver to
their Diocefans annual Lifts of fuch young Perfons belonging to their
Charge, as either are, or might be inftructed in the Duties of Religion, (fpecifying the feveral Impediments or Preventions); This
fingle Circumftance would do more than perhaps at prefent can be
well imagined. Certain it is, That it would give Countenance and
Protection to thofe worthy Clergymen, who are inclined and defirous to do their Duty; and it would fhame and expofe others, if
they did not make the like Returns: Not to mention, that it would

difpofe

diſpoſe the Laity to acquieſce *in,* and to approve *of* ſuch a Regulation, when made a ſtanding Part of their Paſtor's Duty; which otherwiſe, they would cenſure, and object to, and undoubtedly oppoſe, as a peculiar Officiouſneſs, and meddling Temper in *him.* In ſhort, when any Affair is made a regular Part of a Man's Duty, he is never blamed, but rather commended for diſcharging it faithfully: whereas were he to attempt to do the ſame Thing, through any Zeal, or voluntary Act of his own, he would ſoon find, that they would put a very different Conſtruction upon the Matter, and oppoſe him with all their might. —The Paſtors in *North Britain,* as I am informed, are bound by public Authority to go through theſe, or ſuch like annual Examinations, and to make regular Reports to their reſpective Synods. In this they find no Difficulty, but are the more commended and reſpected for it, in Proportion as they uſe the greater Care. And the Morals of the People committed to their Charge, are a ſufficient Proof of the Excellence of the Inſtitution. Why therefore muſt *South Britain* alone be diſtinguiſhed from all the World, wherein, the Inſtitutions of Religion and thoſe of Civil Government concord ſo little with each other?

One general Query more eſpecially adapted for diſcovering the comparative Riches, or Poverty of a Country in paſſing through it.

Q. ARE there any general Rules to be laid down for the Uſe of Travellers to enable them to judge of the comparative Poverty, or Riches of a City, Town, or Country, in paſſing through it?

A. YES there are ſeveral; and ſuch as mutually prove, and corroborate each other:

1. LET the Traveller enquire the relative Price both of Land, and Money; theſe being the certain Criteria of the Riches, or Poverty of a Country; Criteria, like the alternate Buckets of a Well, where the Aſcent of the one neceſſarily ſuppoſes the Deſcent of the other. Thus, for Example, where the Intereſt of Money is high, the Price of Lands muſt be low; becauſe the Height of the Intereſt is a Proof, that there are many to borrow, yet few to lend. And if ſo, then it follows, that wherever there are but few Lenders of Money, there cannot be many Purchaſers of Land. On the contrary, were the Intereſt to be exceeding low, the Price of Lands muſt riſe in Proportion; becauſe the Lowneſs of Intereſt is an infallible Proof, that there are many Perſons in that State capable of making Purchaſes; and yet but few, who want to ſell, or mortgage their Eſtates.

But

But the Effects of high, or low Intereſt are yet to be extended a great deal farther; inaſmuch as the Imployment, or Non-imployment of a People, and conſequently their Riches, or Poverty, will be found to depend in a conſiderable Degree on one, or other of theſe Things. To illuſtrate this, let us ſuppoſe the Intereſt of Money to be low in *England,* as it really is, but high in *France.* Therefore an *Engliſh* Landed Gentleman can afford, and often doth borrow Money on his Eſtate, in order to advance the Value of it, to build, and plant, and make other Improvements: All which give Imployment to the common People, at the ſame Time that they bring clear Gains to himſelf: And the Imployment of a People is their Riches. On the other Hand, a *French* Landed Gentleman cannot afford to do the like; that is, to imploy the People; becauſe the high Intereſt of Money would be greater than his Returns of Profit, or Advantage. Therefore the Eſtates in *France* are in no Degree improved, and advanced in Value like the Eſtates in *England.* And what is here obſerved in regard to the Landed Intereſt, is equally applicable to the Mercantile, and Manufacturing: It being a certain Fact, That a Tradeſman in *France* would rather chuſe to put out his Money to Intereſt (which by the By, creates no Imployment) than be content with thoſe ſmall Profits, which an *Engliſh* Tradeſman is glad to accept of, becauſe he cannot turn his Stock, or Credit to a better Account. — Not to mention, That when a *French* Merchant, or Manufacturer riſes to a Capital of twelve, or fifteen thouſand Pounds, he begins to be ſick, and aſhamed of his Occupation; and will uſe all his Power, and not a little of his Money, to get himſelf and Family ennobled, in order to wipe off the Diſgrace of his original Condition. This being the Caſe, it evidently follows, that the *Engliſh* in general muſt have larger Capitals in Trade than the *French*; and conſequently can, and do employ a greater Number of People in Proportion. Nay, it follows likewiſe, that an *Engliſh* Tradeſman with a Stock of ten thouſand Pounds, will actually underſell his *French* Rival of five thouſand Pounds; even though he ſhould pay dearer for every Article of Work, and Labour. This may ſeem a Paradox to many Perſons, who are unacquainted with Calculations of this Nature: But it can be none to thoſe, who will conſider, that if the *Engliſhman* is content with Five *per Cent.* Profits; while the *Frenchman* expects Eight or Ten *per Cent.* the former may afford to underſell the latter (eſpecially as he hath a double Capital) and yet pay higher Wages to all his Journeymen, and common Tradeſmen.

2. LET

2. L E T the Traveller obferve the Condition of the public Inns on the great Roads: For they likewife are a kind of Pulfe, by which you may difcover the Riches, or Poverty of a Country. If therefore you find them in a flourifhing State, you may depend upon it, that many Paffengers frequent that Road: And the Frequency of Paffing and Re-paffing is a fure Proof, that Bufinefs of fome kind or other is going forwards. The public Inns on the great Roads in *France* are generally bad;—bad, I mean, if compared with the Inns in *England:* Thofe in *Languedoc* are fome of the beft: and if you afk, What is that owing to? It is, becaufe the Trade of *Languedoc* is more confiderable than the Trade of moft other Provinces in the Kingdom.

3. L E T the Traveller make the like Obfervations and Inquiries concerning the Number of Waggons, which pafs and re-pafs the Road.—Waggons never travel for the Sake of Pleafure, but for Ufe: Becaufe their Inducement muft be the Carriage, and confequently the Sale of Goods: And wherever thefe Goods are made, there the People have found Imployment in Proportion.

4. L E T him be particularly attentive to the Quantity and Quality of the Wares to be found in the Shops of the Country Towns, and Villages through which he paffes. For in Fact, fuch Shops are no other than the Magazines of the Place; and by that means become the fureft Indications of the Wealth, or Poverty of the adjacent Neighbourhood. In a Word, rich Cuftomers create rich Shops; but no Shopkeeper will be fo imprudent, as to provide great Stores of valuable Goods, where he can have no reafonable Expectation of vending them. Therefore, let the Traveller, who goes Abroad for the Sake of knowing the State of other Countries, always call at fuch Places, whenever he can have Time: For, a little Money judicioufly laid out in purchafing any Trifle which the Shop affords (though perhaps not worth the carrying to the next Stage) will enable him to make more ufeful Difcoveries, and authorife him to afk more fearching Queftions concerning the Trade, Manufactures, Improvement, or Non-Improvement of the Country, than he could otherwife have done, had he refided whole Months, or even Years among them. And as this is a Fact which the Author may be permitted to fpeak to from his own Experience; therefore he hath a better Right to recommend it to others.

5. L E T the Traveller alfo enquire into the State of Living in Cities and Towns: *viz.* Whether the Inhabitants in general occupy

separate

separate Dwelling-houses; or whether many Families are crouded into one. If the latter is the Case, depend upon it, that the People are poor in Reality, whatever Appearance they put on. For scarce any Family would submit to the Inconvenience of Lodgers, or In-Tenants, if their Circumstances were such, as would enable them to be exempt from it. — Not to mention, that if a Family is to be pent up in a Room or two, the Quantity of Houshold Goods cannot be great: And yet, were a national Inventory to be taken in every Country, the greatest Riches of a State will always be found to consist in Houshold Goods.

6. LET him further observe both in Town and Country, Whether the Generality of the Inhabitants decorate, or keep neat the Outside of their Houses; and bestow some Kind of Ornament on their Grounds and Gardens. For if they do, they certainly are not in distressful Circumstances; the Exterior in this Respect being a sure Proof of the Interior. And the very doing of these Things creates a considerable Quantity of Labour. But, wherever the Houses look decayed or miserable; and the adjacent Gardens and Grounds appear neglected, and Nature lies unimproved; — there you may assure yourself, that the Inhabitants either never felt the Blessing of Prosperity, or have lost it.

7. LASTLY, let him particularly inquire, Whether Tenants in the Country usually pay their Rents in Money, or in Produce. For this is a capital Article in discovering the relative Riches, or Poverty of a Country. If the Rent is paid chiefly, or altogether in Corn, or Cattle; or any the like Productions of the Farm, it is a sure Sign, that Money is exceeding scarce, and that there are no convenient Markets at Hand for the Tenant to sell his Produce, and convert it into Cash. For if there were, neither Landlord, nor Tenant would approve of this Method of Payment, could another be obtained. Not the Landlord, because it would not always suit him to take it in Kind; and because he cannot so conveniently exchange it for other Necessaries or Conveniences: Not the Tenant, because he would certainly prefer a free and open Market for the Sale of his Goods; and would be very unwilling to see the best of his Produce be carried to his Landlord for the Payment of Rent; — nay, in such a Case, he will not think of raising *so good* a Produce, as he other-wise would have done.

AND

AND thus have I ventured, with due Deference to those, whose more immediate Province it may be, to conduct my young Traveller, and to lead him, as it were by the Hand, not only through various Climes, but even through the different Systems of Commerce, Government, and Religion of different Countries. The Manner of doing this, it must be acknowledged, is entirely new; but if the general Method, or Plan proposed is not an improper one; and if some Treatise, or other of this Nature was really wanted; it is humbly hoped, that the Errors and Mistakes of the Author, occasioned by his making his Way over vast, untrodden Grounds, where he had no Guide or Direction, will be looked upon as the more excusable. Indeed, the Apology which will best suit him, and which he is desirous of using on this Occasion; is no other, than what would suit every honest Writer, who hath the Public Good really at Heart, and hopes, that his Labours may at some Time or other, though ever so distant, or in some Degree, though ever so small, be of Use and Advantage to Mankind. That is, he humbly desires, that these Sheets may be considered only as a rude Essay, or the first Attempt of a well-meaning Person on a very important Subject. And if they should prove to be the Means of exciting the superior Abilities of others; or if any Hints here thrown out, shall hereafter be corrected and improved upon; the Design of the Author will be fully answered; and the *Horatian* Motto of *Fungar vice cotis*, will then be his own.

As to the Queries themselves, they are such as may be easily altered, and adapted to the Genius of any Country, People, or Government whatever. And though the young Traveller may at first Sight, be discouraged at their Nature, or Number, as if they would impose a greater Task upon him than he is able, or willing to perform; yet he may assure himself, that the farther he proceeds, the more Delight he will take in these Studies. Moreover, as he is not called upon to hasten, or make any fatiguing Dispatch, but to take Time, and advance gradually, he will find that the Difficulties will lessen every Day; and that these Researches, which at the Beginning perhaps appeared to be a *Labour*, will turn to an *Amusement*. Nay more, seeing that the Questions are already stated (and by that means the great, and perhaps the only real Difficulty taken off his Hands) he will find likewise, that every Person he shall converse with, from the highest to the lowest, will be capable of answering some, or other of these Questions, to his full Content and Satisfaction.

In

IN regard to what the Author hath said particularly about his native Country, the candid and judicious Reader will eafily perceive, that his Defign was neither to commend, nor blame indifcriminately; but to fpeak as impartially as he could, and then, having fet forth, what appeared to him to be the *Truth*, to leave it to operate and take its Courfe. Many great Improvements have been undoubtedly made of late Years in this Kingdom: Yet many more there are ftill to make. And as it would be very difingenuous to deny a Bleffing; it would be equally wrong to conceal a Fault: — Efpecially, if together with the mention of the Fault, a Method is propofed for redreffing it. As to the Times and Seafons, *when* thefe, or fuch like Methods are the propereft to be carried into Execution; that is not the Author's Concern; his Province being only to ftate Facts, and to fubmit Propofals to public Confideration. Perhaps indeed the Time is approaching, and not afar off, when the peculiar Circumftances, and Crifis of Affairs, will require the Adoption of fome of thefe Plans much fooner than could otherwife have been expected. But, be that as it may; when an important Truth is once laid down, it will be perceived to be always growing, though very flow in Growth. *Crefcit occulto velut arbor ævo*, is the Characteriftic of it; and in this, it is juft the Reverfe of Error. Such therefore being the Cafe, may we not hope, that fooner, or later, Truth will certainly prevail? But whether the Author himfelf fhall have the Pleafure of feeing thefe Polities eftablifhed during his own Life-time, is much lefs material, than whether they fhall be eftablifhed at all.

P O S T S C R I P T.

IT is humbly requested of those Gentlemen, and honourable Persons, into whose Hands these Sheets may be committed; that they would please to return them in Two or Three Month's Time, (with their kind Corrections and Amendments in the Margin) sealed up, and delivered either to

The Reverend Dr BIRCH, Secretary to the Royal Society, in *Norfolk-street*, in the *Strand*;

Mr SHIPLEY, at the Society for Arts, Sciences, and Manufactures, at Mr *Fielding*'s Office in the *Strand*;

The Reverend Dr HALES, at *Teddington*, in *Middlesex*; or to

Their most Obliged,

and most Obedient,

humble Servant,

London,
March 24, 1757.

Josiah Tucker,
Rector of St *Stephen*'s in *Bristol*.